I0626876

# Empowered By Resilience:
# A Path to Unstoppable Growth

The Key to Unleashing Your Greatness

by

## Serah W. Muiruri

# DEDICATION

To the Almighty God, the source of all wisdom, strength, and resilience. It is through His boundless grace that I am empowered to overcome every obstacle and continue on this journey of growth and transformation. All glory, honor, and praise belong to You, for You have been my guiding light, my refuge, and my constant companion in this endeavor.

To my beloved parents, Mr. Stephen Muiruri and Mrs. Winnie Muiruri, words cannot fully express my gratitude. Your unwavering love, sacrifices, and support have shaped me into the person I am today. You instilled in me the values of perseverance, faith, and hard work, and for that, I am eternally grateful. You are my foundation, and I dedicate this work to you.

To my siblings—George, Martin, Grace, and Damaris—each of you has been a unique pillar of support, encouragement, and joy in my life. Your love and loyalty inspire me to keep pushing forward, even in the toughest of times. Our bond is unbreakable, and I cherish each of you deeply.

Special thanks to my sister Grace for all the sacrifices you make to ensure the house runs smoothly, especially for those entrusted with our care. This is a true testament to your commitment to humanity! You get to practice your valuable Nursing skills even outside your work. May we never stop sharing love and kindness with those who need it the most.

To my precious nieces and nephews, and especially to Nathan and Nayva Lee, who have shown such keen interest in my journey as an author. Your curiosity and excitement ignite a flame in my heart and remind me why I do what I do. May you always chase your dreams with the same passion and dedication you've shown me.

To my close friends, those who have stood by me through every challenge, celebration, and moment of doubt. Your support has been unwavering, and your belief in me has given me strength when I had none left. To those who have inspired me relentlessly, your encouragement has propelled me forward, and for you, I am eternally grateful.

And a special, heartfelt thank you to my Nonotuck Family. Your unwavering support and love have been a constant source of encouragement, and I am deeply appreciative of the community we share. You have been a family to me in every sense of the word, and your impact on my journey cannot be overstated.

This book is a reflection of all of you—the people who have shaped me, believed in me, and inspired me. It is with immense gratitude and love that I dedicate "Empowered By Resilience: A Path to Unstoppable Growth" to each and every one of you. Thank you for being a part of this journey.

# INTRODUCTION

In a world filled with uncertainty and rapid change, resilience has become more than just a buzzword; it's an essential part of a fulfilling and empowered life. But resilience isn't about simply bouncing back or enduring hardship; it's about transforming those challenges into stepping stones for growth. Resilience is the ultimate key to unlocking your greatness and reaching your unbreakable potential. And this journey isn't just about surviving—it's about thriving.

Not long ago, I found myself standing at a crossroads, overwhelmed by a series of setbacks that left me questioning my path. It was in that moment of doubt that I discovered resilience's true power: a journey that would transform struggles into opportunities and pain into passion. Have you ever felt like life was pushing you down, only to find within yourself a strength you didn't know existed? This book invites you to uncover that inner strength and to see adversity as a catalyst for powerful, personal transformation.

*Empowered by Resilience* will take you step-by-step through the tools and mindsets that will help you navigate life's challenges with confidence. You'll learn how to transform setbacks into comebacks, harness emotional intelligence, and embrace change as an integral part of growth. Each chapter includes actionable exercises, like reflection prompts to help you look back on past challenges, SMART goal-setting to create an achievable vision, and mindfulness techniques to keep you grounded. These practices are designed to

move beyond theory and into daily life, helping you build resilience that's both practical and enduring.

Real-life stories of individuals who turned their challenges into triumphs will remind you that you're not alone on this journey. Whether you're facing relationship issues, career shifts, or personal setbacks, resilience is a skill that you can develop, a skill that transforms struggle into growth and dreams into reality.

This book is more than a guide; it's an invitation to board on a journey toward unstoppable growth. Together, we'll explore how to not only overcome obstacles but also thrive because of them. Resilience is your key to unbreakable potential, and by embracing it, you'll be building a foundation for a life of growth, strength, and success. Let this be the beginning of a journey that transforms challenges into opportunities and ignites a passion for lifelong growth.

# TABLE OF CONTENTS

# Chapter 1:

# From Pain To Passion

*"Pain is inevitable. Suffering is optional."* – Haruki Murakami

Pain is often seen as an antagonist, something we naturally wish to escape. Yet, pain is also a profound paradox, a source of growth and transformation that emerges in the most challenging of life's experiences. Pain disrupts our comfort, yes, but it also sharpens our awareness, urging us to redefine what is possible. It can compel us to reshape our lives in unexpected ways, propelling us toward new paths of purpose and passion. Pain, when approached with courage and perspective, can be more than a burden—it can be a gateway to something greater within us.

The journey from pain to passion is not instantaneous; it's one that requires intentional effort, a willingness to face discomfort, and a commitment to change. The two forces—pain and passion—exist on a continuum, often feeding into one another in a way that can feel disorienting, even contradictory. Pain leaves us with scars, both visible and invisible, and sometimes, those scars seem to act as constant reminders of what we've endured. But over time, they can also act as symbols of resilience, testaments to our ability to move forward. The lessons embedded in our struggles teach us not only to endure but to channel our experiences into something meaningful.

And as we do so, we begin to see that the path through pain often leads us to a place of clarity, purpose, and passion.

The dichotomy between pain and passion forms the cornerstone of this journey. To move from one to the other requires a shift in perspective, a readiness to see pain not just as an enemy but as a catalyst for growth. This shift doesn't deny the reality of suffering— it honors it, allowing it to guide us toward a deeper understanding of ourselves and the world around us.

In this chapter, we explore how this transformation unfolds, examining how pain can evolve into purpose and how embracing passion can redefine our experiences, offering us not only hope but a new, empowered identity.

## Pain & Environment

Pain isn't always the product of a single, isolated event. It often lingers, woven into the fabric of our daily lives through small, repeated experiences, unkind words, or unfulfilled expectations. To transform pain into passion, we first need to understand it as a complex, multi-layered experience. The initial goal in studying this journey is to recognize the interplay between pain and passion—two forces that seem incompatible yet are deeply intertwined. Pain strips us down to our core, exposing vulnerabilities we may have concealed even from ourselves. It challenges us to confront what we truly believe, reshaping our internal landscape and pushing us to examine how we respond to life's hardships.

At its root, this transformation requires us to modify our environment. The environment here refers to both our internal and external worlds—our thoughts, beliefs, and behaviors, as well as the spaces we inhabit, the people we surround ourselves with, and the situations we put ourselves in. Pain can compel us to re-evaluate these elements, identifying those that no longer serve us and replacing them with ones that encourage healing and growth. This is not always easy; it often requires breaking habits, altering mindsets, and letting go of attachments. Yet, these changes can cultivate an environment that nurtures passion rather than stifles it.

To modify our environment is to take ownership of our lives and to become active participants in our own healing. It's about fostering spaces that reflect our values and aspirations, places where we can explore and develop our passions without fear of judgment. By intentionally curating both our physical and mental surroundings, we create a foundation upon which transformation can thrive. It's here, within this consciously designed environment, that the seeds of passion are sown, nurtured by a willingness to embrace the lessons pain has taught us.

## Pain as Paradox: The Transformative Conflict

The nature of pain as a paradox lies in its ability to both hinder and empower. Pain brings discomfort, often challenging our sense of security and stability. Yet, within that very discomfort lies the opportunity for growth. Pain confronts us with conflict—the conflict between who we are and who we aspire to be, between our limitations and our potential, between our fears and our courage. It's a conflict

that may feel destabilizing, but it's also one that pushes us beyond complacency, urging us to redefine our lives.

Personal transformation isn't a linear process, nor is it a simple one. Pain forces us to navigate a landscape filled with contradictions. On one hand, we long to escape it; on the other, we recognize that there are valuable lessons hidden within it. This paradox—the tension between suffering and growth—requires us to balance acceptance with action. Accepting pain doesn't mean we resign ourselves to suffering; rather, it means acknowledging our experiences and understanding their impact on us. From this place of acceptance, we can then take action, transforming our pain into a driving force for positive change.

The ideology of pain as a transformative conflict reveals that suffering doesn't diminish us; it deepens us. It compels us to redefine our boundaries, values, and priorities. In doing so, we begin to view pain not merely as a source of hardship but as a stepping stone toward a more profound understanding of our capabilities. This perspective allows us to see the potential for passion within our suffering, enabling us to transform our experiences into something constructive and fulfilling.

**Modifying Our Thought Patterns: A Path to Lasting Change**

The mind has a tendency to cling to pain, often replaying past hurts and magnifying present struggles. To move from pain to passion, we must address these patterns of thinking, identifying those that perpetuate suffering and replacing them with perspectives that foster resilience. This process doesn't happen overnight; it requires consistent effort and

a commitment to self-awareness. Yet, by actively choosing to reinterpret our experiences, we begin to reshape our relationship with pain, transforming it from an oppressive force into one that empowers us.

One effective method of modifying negative thought patterns is through cognitive reframing, a process that involves consciously shifting our perspective on painful experiences. Rather than seeing pain as an obstacle, we can choose to view it as a teacher, a source of insight and growth. This doesn't mean ignoring or denying our suffering; rather, it means choosing to interpret it in a way that serves our growth. By reframing our thoughts, we empower ourselves to move beyond victimhood, stepping into a role where we actively shape our reality.

Another powerful tool in changing our thought patterns is the practice of mindfulness. Mindfulness encourages us to observe our thoughts without judgment, allowing us to see our pain with clarity rather than resistance. Through mindfulness, we learn to accept our experiences as they are without letting them define us. This practice cultivates a sense of inner peace, enabling us to move through pain with grace and resilience. As we become more mindful, we develop the ability to respond to life's challenges with calm and clarity, transforming our pain into a source of strength.

**Cultivating Passion: The Power of Purpose**

Passion is the force that emerges when we find purpose in our pain. It's the fire that propels us forward, giving us the strength to rise above our struggles and pursue something meaningful. Passion

doesn't erase pain, but it gives it direction, channeling our experiences into pursuits that align with our values and aspirations. This process of cultivating passion is deeply personal and unique to each individual's journey and perspective. It's not about finding a single, definitive purpose; it's about discovering the passions that make life vibrant and fulfilling.

For some, this passion may manifest as a dedication to helping others, using personal experiences to support and inspire those facing similar challenges. For others, it may take the form of creative expression, a means of articulating emotions that words alone cannot capture. Whatever the form, passion allows us to transform pain into purpose, giving us a reason to persevere even when circumstances seem bleak. By aligning our lives with our passions, we create a path forward, one that honors our experiences and allows us to grow.

The journey from pain to passion is ultimately a journey of self-discovery. It's about learning to embrace our imperfections, honoring our struggles, and finding meaning in our experiences. When we cultivate passion, we're not just overcoming pain—we're integrating it, allowing it to shape us into stronger, more compassionate individuals. Through this process, we gain a deeper understanding of ourselves and the world around us, recognizing that pain, while challenging, can also be a source of profound growth and transformation.

## Methods for Lasting Transformation

The journey from pain to passion doesn't end with a single revelation; it's a continuous process of growth and refinement. To support this journey, it's essential to explore practical methods for maintaining positive change and preventing relapse into old patterns of negativity. Here is a table of some approaches that can facilitate lasting transformation:

| Method | Description | Benefit |
|---|---|---|
| Cognitive Behavioral Techniques (CBT) | CBT helps identify and challenge negative thought patterns, replacing them with empowering beliefs. Effective for overcoming self-limiting beliefs. | Builds confidence and resilience by reshaping negative thinking into a more constructive outlook. |
| Journaling and Reflection | Writing down thoughts and experiences provides clarity and emotional release, allowing for self-reflection and progress acknowledgment. | Enhances self-awareness, fosters emotional healing, and provides a record of personal growth. |
| Setting SMART Goals | Establishes Specific, Measurable, Achievable, Relevant, and Time-bound goals to structure aspirations into clear steps. | Encourages motivation, provides direction, and breaks down large goals into manageable actions. |
| Affirmations and Visualization | Positive affirmations reinforce belief in overcoming challenges, while visualization aligns focus with future passions. | Strengthens goal focus, promotes a positive mindset, and supports resilience through mental rehearsal. |
| Mindfulness and Meditation | Practicing mindfulness cultivates peace, while meditation enhances self-awareness and nonjudgmental emotional navigation. | Promotes emotional stability, reduces stress, and strengthens resilience in challenging situations. |

*"What lies behind us and what lies before us are tiny matters compared to what lies within us."* – **Ralph Waldo Emerson**

Pain and passion may appear as opposing forces, but within the tension between them lies the potential for transformation. By learning to embrace pain, reframing our experiences, and cultivating passion, we can create a life that not only honors our struggles but also celebrates our resilience. The journey from pain to passion is a challenging one, but it's a journey that ultimately leads us to a place of strength, purpose, and fulfillment.

# Chapter 2:

# In the Eye of the Storm

*"Resilience is not just about bouncing back, but growing stronger in the face of adversity."*

Resilience is often imagined as a fortress—an unbreakable shield against life's storms. But true resilience is more fluid, like water that finds its way around obstacles, adapting and moving forward no matter the force against it. Resilience is felt deep within as an unwavering belief that no matter the chaos surrounding us, we have the inner resources to face it. This strength often lies hidden until life calls upon it, bringing to light a power we might not have recognized before. In those moments of turbulence, resilience is not only our response to adversity; it's our ability to remain steady within it, learning to see even the eye of the storm as a place of potential growth.

To many, resilience feels like a quiet determination—a feeling that goes beyond willpower or mere grit. It's a process shaped by moments of doubt, struggle, and vulnerability, reminding us that strength lies not only in pushing forward but in knowing when to bend, to pause, and to reflect. This adaptability allows us to face challenges not with resistance but with openness to learn and evolve. Each storm, each setback, teaches us to build our inner core stronger and wiser.

Yet, resilience is also a journey—a path of trust in oneself and in the unknown. There's an element of surrender that weaves through resilience, teaching us that not every answer lies in control and not every struggle needs to be understood in the moment. As we navigate the uncertainties, we learn to let go of what we cannot control and, instead, focus on what we can. This chapter explores that journey—the roadmap to resilience through turbulence—and the practices that fortify our ability to trust ourselves even in the midst of life's most unpredictable storms.

**The Roadmap to Resilience from Turbulence**

Navigating turbulence isn't about ignoring the challenges or bypassing the struggle; it's about recognizing the storm as part of our growth journey. Resilience asks us to shift our perspective and see these moments as experiences that can reshape us for the better. We'll explore key practices and mindsets that help us not only endure the storm but emerge from it stronger and more capable.

**Trusting the Journey**

Trust is foundational to resilience. In moments of turbulence, it's natural to want immediate solutions or certainty. But resilience teaches us that sometimes the most significant growth happens when we trust the journey, even when we can't see the path clearly. Developing trust allows us to stay grounded in the present, enabling us to respond calmly and thoughtfully to whatever comes our way.

# Roadmap to Resilience: Tools for Managing the Unknown

| Tool | Description | How to Use | Benefit |
|---|---|---|---|
| **Grounding Techniques** | Practices that bring focus to the present moment and reduce anxiety about the future or past. | Try deep breathing exercises, mindful observation, or sensory grounding (e.g., focusing on textures). | Reduces stress and increases calm in the face of challenges. |
| **Journaling** | Writing down thoughts to process emotions and gain perspective on difficult situations. | Use prompts like "What is in my control?" or "What am I learning from this?" | Encourages clarity and helps in reframing negative thoughts. |
| **Acceptance Practices** | Acknowledging what can't be changed, allowing energy to be directed toward actionable solutions. | Reflect on challenges that are beyond your control and focus on response rather than reaction. | Builds mental flexibility and conserves emotional energy. |
| **Self-Compassion** | Treating oneself with kindness, especially during setbacks. | Practice self-kindness by acknowledging effort over outcomes and celebrating small victories. | Boosts resilience by fostering a supportive inner dialogue. |
| **Positive Reframing** | Shifting perspective to find lessons or potential growth in challenging experiences. | Ask yourself, "How can this experience contribute to my growth?" | Increases adaptability and builds an optimistic outlook. |

**Building a Resilient Mindset Amidst Turbulence**

One of resilience's greatest teachings is that adversity often presents unexpected gifts. When we encounter setbacks, they challenge our current perspectives, offering opportunities to realign with our values, goals, and personal growth. This realignment is the heart of a resilient mindset, as it transforms obstacles into stepping stones for growth.

The practices outlined here aim to cultivate this mindset by encouraging us to examine our reactions to adversity and explore how we can adapt positively. Let's explore some of the core tools that enable resilience, fostering a mindset prepared to face and even embrace turbulence.

**1. Self-Awareness:**

Resilience begins with self-awareness. This is the ability to observe our thoughts, feelings, and reactions without judgment. Self-awareness allows us to recognize patterns that may either help or hinder our resilience. By regularly checking in with ourselves, we gain insight into how we respond to stress, allowing us to make conscious choices about how to move forward.

*"In the waves of change, we find our true direction."*

**2. Flexibility**

A resilient mindset is flexible. Rather than resisting change, resilience teaches us to approach it with curiosity. Flexibility allows us to adapt to life's unpredictability, seeing each change as an opportunity to grow. This approach helps us stay open to new paths and solutions,

12

reducing the anxiety that can come from wanting things to remain the same.

**Case Study:**

**Trusting the Unknown**

*"Imagine Deborah, a teacher who recently lost her job due to unexpected school closures. Initially, Deborah felt devastated, her identity and stability shaken. But after giving herself space to grieve, she began exploring her long-time interest in graphic design. She took an online course, refined her skills, and eventually landed a job in a field she'd never considered before. Through resilience, Deborah discovered a passion that might have remained hidden had she not trusted the unknown."*

This example highlights how resilience invites us to trust the journey and remain open to opportunities that arise, even if they are far from our original plans.

## Tools for Managing the Unknown

Resilience is strengthened through intentional practices that anchor us when life feels chaotic. Here are additional tools to help manage the unknown:

| Tool | Description | How to Use | Benefit |
|---|---|---|---|
| **Visualization Exercises** | Imagining successful outcomes to build confidence in facing challenges. | Close your eyes and picture yourself overcoming the current situation. Visualize your strengths in action. | Reduces fear by focusing on positive outcomes. |
| **Resilience Check-Ins** | Regularly assessing one's mental and emotional state during prolonged challenges. | Create a checklist to track feelings, needs, and coping strategies. | Builds self-awareness and tracks personal growth. |
| **Physical Activity** | Engaging in exercise to release tension and build mental and emotional endurance. | Go for a walk, try yoga, or engage in any preferred physical activity. | Reduces stress and improves emotional resilience. |
| **Support Systems** | Connecting with mentors, peers, or loved ones who provide guidance and encouragement. | Schedule regular check-ins with supportive individuals. | Reinforces resilience by offering perspective and motivation. |

Resilience isn't just an abstract concept; it's an active process shaped by the choices we make each day. Each tool, from grounding techniques to resilience check-ins, is a step toward building a mindset that can weather any storm. When we embrace resilience, we're not

only preparing ourselves to endure life's challenges but transforming each experience into a stepping stone for personal growth.

*"Strength doesn't come from what you can do; it comes from overcoming the things you once thought you couldn't."*

This chapter has shown how resilience helps us navigate uncertainty by trusting in ourselves and the journey. The tools and practices shared here are not only ways to endure adversity but to actively engage with it, finding purpose and strength within life's inevitable storms. By embracing resilience, we build a foundation that allows us to thrive amidst turbulence, transforming each challenge into a step toward our greatest potential.

# Chapter 3:

# The Resilient Journey

*"Resilience is not a single act of strength, but a journey of persistent growth and rediscovery."*

### Realizing One's True Potential; Resilience Redefined

The journey toward resilience is rarely straightforward, but its rewards are unmatched. Resilience isn't just the act of standing firm against life's storms; it's a continual process of growth that takes shape with each decision, each struggle, and each new perspective. As we engage with resilience, we often find that it doesn't simply mean bouncing back to who we were before a challenge but evolving into a version of ourselves we might not have previously imagined. This transformative path reveals to us the layers of our strength and potential—qualities that only emerge under pressure and serve as evidence of our remarkable capacity to endure, learn, and thrive. Every moment we choose resilience, we uncover a bit more of our true potential, redefining it in ways that wouldn't be possible without adversity.

Resilience, redefined, is fluid, evolving as we grow and adapt to life's changes. Traditional definitions of resilience might bring to mind rigid strength or unwavering resolve. However, true resilience is more like water than stone, adapting to the terrain rather than resisting it. Our ability to persist through challenges and embrace change is fueled by self-awareness and a willingness to redefine who we are in response to

our environment. Resilience urges us to release preconceived limitations and invites us to see potential in places we may have once dismissed. It teaches us that each hurdle is not a permanent barrier but a temporary gateway to new understanding. Through this journey, resilience reshapes itself and, in doing so, reshapes us.

Realizing our true potential through resilience requires a mindset that is open, introspective, and curious. It is tempting to think of ourselves as static, to accept that who we are at any moment is all we are capable of becoming. However, resilience breaks down these barriers by showing us that self-perception is as adaptable as the circumstances around us. In facing struggles, we learn not only our strengths but also areas where we can grow. This understanding becomes a valuable tool in our journey; for it offers us a roadmap to cultivate strengths, we may not have initially recognized. Resilience isn't about being impenetrable; it's about embracing our vulnerabilities and finding power within them. This journey encourages us to dig deep, redefining potential in each step we take, trusting that every choice we make builds the resilience necessary to handle life's challenges.

To embark on the journey of resilience is to commit to growth without fully knowing the destination. Often, we are guided by the trials we face, discovering strength only as we encounter obstacles. Resilience calls us to redefine purpose and find alignment within ourselves. It's not simply about overcoming adversity; it's about seeing the resilience journey as a continuous dialogue with our potential. This dialogue doesn't end after one challenge; it is an ongoing conversation with

ourselves. Through resilience, we learn that our potential is dynamic, always moving and reshaping itself to meet us where we are. Each challenge invites us to see ourselves more fully and to recognize the capabilities that have quietly resided within us, waiting to be realized.

Resilience and potential are woven together, shaping the roadmap of our lives. Our challenges become the milestones that reflect not just our ability to endure but our capacity to redefine ourselves along the way. Resilience is both the compass that guides us forward and the evolving map that tracks our growth. We may not always understand why we encounter certain challenges, but each one reveals a new dimension of who we are. The beauty of resilience lies in its adaptability—it shapes itself to each experience, each triumph, and each setback. This journey through resilience becomes a powerful testament to our inner strength and our untapped potential, revealing to us that we are capable of far more than we once thought.

As we journey through life, resilience continually asks us to rise beyond limitations and embrace our highest potential. It requires courage to face difficult times, but in doing so, we awaken new parts of ourselves. Resilience doesn't remove hardship from our path, but it empowers us to face it with greater strength and clarity. Our potential isn't a fixed state; it's a constantly evolving landscape that resilience helps us navigate. Every time we choose growth, every time we embrace change, we strengthen our resolve. This ongoing journey reveals that resilience isn't merely an end state; it's a practice—a deliberate choice to build a life rooted in purpose, passion, and unyielding strength.

## Personal Development is a Fluid and Ongoing Process

Personal development is not a one-time achievement but a fluid process that continuously evolves. As we move through life, resilience serves as a guide, reminding us that growth doesn't follow a straight line. There will be times when progress feels slow and moments when it feels rapid. This ebb and flow is natural and should be embraced as part of the journey. Resilience teaches us that we can allow ourselves to grow at our own pace, trusting that every experience contributes to our development. Personal growth thrives on resilience, finding its rhythm in the moments of self-reflection, adaptability, and renewal that shape our perspective over time. By committing to this ongoing process, we allow ourselves the freedom to transform continuously, guided by resilience in each phase.

This fluid approach to personal development fosters self-compassion, encouraging us to approach each challenge with an open mind. Resilience reminds us that setbacks are not failures but rather opportunities to learn and realign with our true potential. Each moment of growth is an invitation to explore the parts of ourselves we may have previously overlooked. Through resilience, we learn that personal development is not about becoming someone else; it's about becoming a fuller, more authentic version of ourselves. This journey requires patience, curiosity, and a belief that every experience, no matter how small, contributes to our broader sense of purpose and achievement.

## Tools for Self-Analysis: Recognizing Growth Through Reflection

Below is a table of self-analysis tools that can aid in the process of personal growth, with a focus on building resilience:

| Tool | Purpose | Steps | Benefits |
| --- | --- | --- | --- |
| **Reflective Journaling** | To gain clarity on thoughts, emotions, and growth areas | Write down daily or weekly reflections on challenges, successes, and lessons learned. Review entries periodically for recurring patterns. | Enhances self-awareness and helps track growth over time. |
| **SWOT Analysis** | To assess personal strengths, weaknesses, opportunities, and threats | Divide a journal page into four sections: Strengths, Weaknesses, Opportunities, and Threats. List relevant points for each category. | Provides a clear framework for recognizing potential growth areas and areas needing improvement. |
| **Goal-Setting Exercises** | To set realistic, achievable growth targets | Use SMART criteria (Specific, Measurable, Achievable, Relevant, Time-bound) to outline short- and long-term goals. | Fosters a sense of direction and motivation to reach desired outcomes. |
| **Mind Mapping** | To visualize and organize thoughts around personal growth | Start with a central idea (like "My Growth") and branch out with key areas, challenges, goals, and resources related to personal development. | Encourages creativity and a holistic view of the journey toward self-improvement. |
| **Feedback Review** | To seek constructive insights from others | Request feedback from trusted mentors or peers. Note insights, and reflect on how you can apply their suggestions to improve. | Offers external perspectives and promotes accountability in the growth process. |

Incorporating these tools into the journey of resilience allows for consistent self-analysis and reinforces the message that growth is continuous and flexible. By regularly engaging in reflective practices, we empower ourselves to recognize areas of success and focus on aspects that need nurturing. With resilience as our guide, we stay motivated, always ready to adapt and advance on our personal development path.

*"The journey of resilience is paved with self-discovery, persistence, and the courage to embrace who you are becoming."*

This chapter has taught us that resilience is not a fixed trait but a fluid and ongoing process. We explored how personal development unfolds through introspection and the redefinition of resilience as a journey rather than a destination. Through practical tools for self-analysis and strategies to unlock our true potential, this chapter inspires us to embrace growth as a lifelong commitment.

# Chapter 4:

# Opening New Ways For

# Personal Development

*"Challenges are not stop signs; they are guidelines."* – Robert H.
Schuller.

**Perseverance, Self-Improvement, Increased Awareness, Hurdle
Overcoming, Dosage**

Challenges are an inevitable part of life, acting as stepping stones to
personal development. They test our resolve, demand our attention, and
stretch our limits. Perseverance—the ability to endure and push forward
despite difficulties—is not just a virtue but a transformative practice.
Through challenges, we are invited to shed the familiar and embrace
growth, even when it feels uncomfortable or uncertain. Life's hurdles are
often cloaked in discomfort, yet they hold the keys to deeper
understanding and self-improvement. They call on us to rise above fear,
to learn from every stumble, and to see each obstacle as an opportunity
to rewrite our narrative. Perseverance isn't about avoiding failure but
about learning how to navigate it and come out stronger on the other side.

Self-improvement begins with acknowledging challenges as catalysts
for growth. Each obstacle presents a chance to learn, adapt, and redefine
our perspectives. It's easy to feel disheartened when faced with

difficulty, but moments of struggle often bring clarity, helping us identify areas where we need to improve. Increased awareness—a critical component of personal growth—emerges when we confront challenges head-on. By analyzing our reactions, choices, and patterns, we uncover insights that were previously hidden. This self-awareness allows us to fine-tune our approach to life, cultivating habits and mindsets that propel us forward. Challenges, then, are not merely barriers; they are mirrors reflecting the parts of us that are ready to grow.

Overcoming hurdles requires both strategy and mindset. While some challenges may seem insurmountable, breaking them down into smaller, manageable steps can make them less intimidating. This process, often referred to as "dosage," involves taking gradual, consistent actions toward a larger goal. Just as a small dose of medicine administered over time leads to healing, taking incremental steps helps us build resilience and achieve progress. Hurdles teach us patience and persistence, emphasizing the importance of consistency over immediate results. By approaching challenges with a dose-by-dose mindset, we transform them from overwhelming mountains into a series of achievable steps, reinforcing our ability to persevere.

Challenges also serve as a training ground for resilience, sharpening our problem-solving skills and expanding our capacity for creative thinking. When faced with adversity, we are forced to look beyond conventional solutions, finding new ways to approach old problems. This increased awareness fosters innovation, helping us to adapt to changing circumstances with greater ease. Each challenge we

overcome builds a foundation for future success, instilling confidence in our ability to handle whatever comes our way. Over time, we learn that life's obstacles are not meant to hinder us but to shape us, refining our character and deepening our understanding of ourselves.

Ultimately, perseverance through life's challenges opens new pathways for self-discovery and fulfillment. By embracing the struggle, we tap into our inner strength and uncover potential we may not have realized existed. Challenges force us to confront our limitations, but they also reveal the boundless possibilities within us. Each difficulty we face teaches us something new—about the world, about others, and most importantly, about ourselves. Through perseverance, we transform life's hardships into stepping stones for growth, healing, and meaningful pursuits. It is in the face of adversity that we truly come to understand the depth of our resilience and the power of our determination.

**Chase the difficulties in life as they convert the struggles into growth, healing, and meaningful life pursuits.**

Life's difficulties are often seen as interruptions to our happiness, but they are, in fact, the catalysts for transformation. Each struggle we encounter carries the potential to reshape us, redirecting our focus toward growth and healing. Chasing these difficulties—rather than avoiding them—requires a shift in mindset. It means recognizing that pain and hardship are not to be feared but embraced as tools for personal evolution. Just as pressure turns coal into diamonds, challenges refine our character, enhancing our ability to navigate life

with purpose and strength. By leaning into the discomfort of life's struggles, we unlock the door to a more meaningful existence.

Growth often arises from discomfort, as it pushes us to confront areas of our lives that need change or improvement. When we chase life's difficulties, we are not seeking pain for its own sake but pursuing the lessons and opportunities it brings. Each challenge becomes a stepping stone toward a better version of ourselves, offering insights that only adversity can reveal. Healing, too, is often a byproduct of facing struggles. Through challenges, we learn to release what no longer serves us, making space for new perspectives, habits, and connections. The process of overcoming difficulties helps us align with our true purpose, guiding us toward pursuits that bring fulfillment and joy.

Meaningful life pursuits are born out of the resilience we build through challenges. When we chase difficulties, we are, in essence, chasing growth. We are actively seeking the opportunities that lie hidden within the struggle, choosing to see life's hurdles not as barriers but as bridges to something greater. This perspective allows us to approach challenges with curiosity rather than fear, fostering a sense of empowerment and purpose. Over time, this mindset becomes a way of life, encouraging us to view every obstacle as an invitation to grow, heal, and connect with what truly matters.

In the end, the pursuit of life's difficulties leads us to a deeper understanding of ourselves and the world around us. It teaches us that struggles are not setbacks but stepping stones, guiding us toward our highest potential. Each challenge we face adds to the richness of our

journey, reminding us that life's true beauty lies not in its ease but in its complexity. By chasing life's difficulties, we become active participants in our own growth, choosing to transform pain into purpose and hardship into healing. This journey is not always easy, but it is always worth it.

**Activities, Motivational Accounts, and Tips for Growth**

1. **(First Activity)**: *Gratitude Journaling for Challenges*

   o **Purpose**: To reframe challenges as opportunities for growth.

   o **Instructions**: Each day, write down one challenge you faced and one lesson or strength it helped you uncover. Over time, review your entries to see how your mindset shifts.

   o **Outcome**: Encourages a positive perspective on difficulties and builds resilience.

2. **(Motivational Account)**: *The Marathon Runner's Story*

   o A young woman trains for her first marathon, struggling through injuries and self-doubt. Despite setbacks, she perseveres, learning to listen to her body and trust the process. When she finally crosses the finish line, she realizes that the journey—not the race—was the true victory.

3. **(Growth Tip)**: *The Power of Reflection*

   o Spend 10 minutes each evening reflecting on the day's challenges. Ask yourself: "What did this teach me?" and "How can I use this lesson tomorrow?"

4. **(Growth Tip)**: *Small Wins Lead to Big Changes*

   o Celebrate every small victory, no matter how minor it seems. Small wins compound over time, building confidence and momentum for larger achievements.

## Tools for Expanding Outlook

| Tool | Purpose | Steps | Benefits |
|---|---|---|---|
| **Mindfulness Practices** | To stay present and reduce stress during challenges | Dedicate 10 minutes daily to meditation or deep breathing. Focus on grounding yourself in the present moment. | Enhances emotional clarity and reduces anxiety during turbulent times. |
| **Visualization Exercises** | To envision solutions and outcomes | Close your eyes and picture a challenge resolved. Imagine the steps you took and how it feels to succeed. | Boosts motivation and helps clarify actionable steps toward goals. |
| **Networking and Support** | To seek help and diverse perspectives | Share your challenges with trusted friends, mentors, or support groups. Gather advice and encouragement. | Fosters a sense of community and provides practical solutions to complex problems. |
| **Continuous Learning** | To stay adaptable and informed | Read books, attend workshops, or take online courses related to personal development and resilience. | Expands knowledge and equips you with tools for overcoming hurdles. |
| **Affirmations and Reframing** | To shift negative thoughts into positive ones | Write down affirmations like, "I am capable of handling this," and repeat them when challenges arise. Reframe setbacks as opportunities. | Builds confidence and fosters a growth-oriented mindset. |

The challenges we face in life are not meant to defeat us but to strengthen us. They are the training grounds for perseverance, the catalysts for self-improvement, and the gateways to a richer, more fulfilling existence. By embracing life's difficulties with curiosity and courage, we transform struggle into growth, pain into purpose, and adversity into opportunity. Through perseverance and resilience, we unlock the limitless potential within us, paving the way for a journey filled with healing, growth, and meaning.

**"It is not the mountain we conquer, but ourselves." – Sir Edmund Hillary.**

This chapter has taught us that life's challenges are not barriers but opportunities for growth, healing, and personal development. Through perseverance, we build resilience, sharpen our problem-solving skills, and deepen our self-awareness. By embracing difficulties, we unlock our potential to overcome adversity and transform pain into purpose. The tools, activities, and motivational insights provided here are stepping stones to cultivating a growth-oriented mindset. Remember, each challenge we face is a chance to strengthen our character and enrich our life journey.

*"Difficulties strengthen the mind, as labor does the body." – Seneca*

# Chapter 5:

# The Resilient Revolution

*"The greatest revolution in our generation is the discovery that human beings, by changing the inner attitudes of their minds, can change the outer aspects of their lives."* – William James.

*Transformation from Within; Adaptation*

**Understanding the Core of Transformation**

Transformation begins with a choice. It is the conscious decision to break away from stagnant patterns and redefine our perspective. At its heart lies adaptation—our ability to navigate change with grace and purpose. Life's unpredictable waves often leave us at a crossroads, urging us to either resist or evolve. True transformation requires both courage and flexibility, an unwavering commitment to move forward despite uncertainty.

As individuals, we thrive when we align with our inner compass, challenging old beliefs while embracing new perspectives. Transformation from within is less about external success and more about achieving harmony with ourselves. It's about peeling back the layers of doubt and fear to reveal the unshakable foundation of resilience that lies beneath.

## The Power of Adaptation

Adaptation is the cornerstone of resilience. The more we adapt, the more fluidly we can respond to life's demands. Think of it as a muscle: the more we practice, the stronger it becomes. Adaptation involves accepting change, redefining priorities, and envisioning a new way forward.

In history, revolutions are marked by a radical shift in thought or action. Similarly, the resilient revolution within us begins with a decision to embrace change. Each step, no matter how small, contributes to the profound journey of self-discovery. Adaptation is not about perfection; it's about progress. By learning to adapt, we master the art of staying grounded even when the winds of change blow strongest.

## Revolutionizing Your Inner World

The transformation from within doesn't happen overnight. It involves rewiring thoughts, challenging limiting beliefs and committing to self-awareness. Start by identifying the patterns that no longer serve you. Are there habits or thought processes keeping you stagnant? Revolutionizing your inner world begins when you confront these barriers with honesty and compassion.

Journaling is a powerful tool to achieve this. Through daily reflections, you can track your growth, acknowledge your struggles, and redefine your aspirations. Over time, you'll notice a shift: your mind becomes clearer, your actions more intentional, and your resilience more profound.

## The Role of Support Systems in Transformation

No revolution is won alone. Surrounding yourself with a supportive network accelerates your transformation. Whether it's family, friends, mentors, or professional support, these connections provide strength during times of doubt. They remind you that you're not alone and that others have walked similar paths.

However, the ultimate revolution lies within. While external support is invaluable, true transformation happens when you trust yourself to rise, adapt, and thrive. It's a collaborative journey, but the responsibility to grow rests with you.

### *Key Message: Self-awareness and Resilience*

### Resilience: A Lifelong Practice

Resilience is not just a quality; it's a way of life, a philosophy that integrates endurance, adaptability, and the wisdom gained through experience. Think of resilience as a muscle that grows stronger each time it is stretched. Life will present obstacles, and how we respond to those challenges determines the trajectory of our personal growth.

At its core, resilience is the ability to endure hardship without losing sight of hope and purpose. It's the strength to keep going when the path ahead seems unclear. However, resilience isn't just about surviving tough times—it's about thriving because of them. Every setback is an opportunity to "bounce forward," not just back to where you started. This forward movement is what distinguishes resilience as a lifelong practice.

By cultivating self-awareness, we unlock the key to resilience. Self-awareness enables us to recognize our triggers, understand our coping mechanisms, and assess our emotional and mental states. This understanding serves as the foundation upon which personal growth is built, giving us the ability to navigate life's storms with clarity and confidence.

## The Mirror of Self-Awareness

Self-awareness is the cornerstone of resilience. It acts as a mirror, reflecting our thoughts, emotions, and actions. This reflection provides the clarity needed to take control of our lives rather than being reactive to circumstances. Self-awareness allows us to observe our habits and patterns, helping us identify what works and what hinders our growth.

Developing self-awareness is a transformative process. It requires us to confront uncomfortable truths about ourselves—our fears, insecurities, and limitations. This confrontation, while challenging, is the first step in breaking free from the constraints of old patterns. For instance, if a person tends to retreat in the face of criticism, self-awareness might reveal the underlying fear of inadequacy. With this insight, they can consciously work to address and overcome this fear, fostering resilience in the process.

Through self-awareness, we also develop emotional intelligence, the ability to understand and manage our emotions and those of others. Emotional intelligence enhances our relationships and strengthens our

capacity to adapt to change. It empowers us to respond to life's challenges with composure and purpose, building a resilient mindset that evolves over time.

**Tools for Building Resilience Through Awareness**

Building resilience requires practical tools that bridge intention with action. Journaling, meditation, and mindfulness exercises are effective practices for fostering self-awareness. Dedicate time each day to explore your thoughts and emotions, acknowledging both your victories and setbacks.

A structured journaling approach over four weeks can serve as a roadmap for self-discovery and resilience building. Begin by setting clear intentions and track your progress over time.

**4. Practical Application: The Four-Week Journaling Plan**

| Week | Focus | Activity | Benefit |
|------|-------|----------|---------|
| Week 1 | Self-Reflection | Write about your challenges and successes daily. | Builds self-awareness and emotional clarity. |
| Week 2 | Identifying Strengths | Note down moments where you displayed resilience. | Reinforces positive self-belief. |
| Week 3 | Overcoming Limitations | Explore habits or thoughts that hold you back. | Identifies areas for growth. |
| Week 4 | Vision for the Future | Set goals for personal and professional growth. | Encourages forward-thinking and optimism. |

**Special Notes: Inner Explorations—Four-Week Journaling**

**How to Use Journaling for Growth**

Journaling is more than writing; it's a conversation with yourself. Use it to delve into your emotions, explore your dreams, and confront your fears. The act of putting pen to paper clarifies thoughts and helps process experiences. Over time, it becomes a powerful tool for resilience and personal growth.

**Motivational Accounts and Tips**

- **The Story of Maya Angelou**: Despite facing immense challenges, Angelou's resilience and self-awareness transformed her into an iconic figure of hope and strength.

- **Tip**: Start small. Dedicate five minutes daily to journaling. Consistency matters more than duration.

- **Tip**: Use prompts like "What am I grateful for today?" or "What challenge did I overcome recently?" to guide your reflections.

**Final Thoughts on Inner Explorations**

Inner exploration isn't about perfection; it's about progress. Be patient with yourself as you navigate this journey. Celebrate your growth, no matter how small, and trust the process.

*"The journey of a thousand miles begins with one step." –*
**Lao Tzu.**

This chapter has taught us that resilience is not a one-time achievement but an ongoing revolution within ourselves. Transformation begins with self-awareness and adaptation, and it's through this journey that we unlock our true potential. The tools and insights shared here encourage a structured approach to growth, empowering us to face challenges with clarity and confidence. Remember, the greatest revolutions are those that happen within as we align with our purpose and embrace life's uncertainties.

*"Success is not final, failure is not fatal: It is the courage to continue that count." – Winston Churchill.*

# Chapter 6:

# Healing the Wounds

*"The wound is the place where the light enters you."* – Rumi.

**The Silent Struggles of Mental Health**

Mental health is often referred to as the silent epidemic—a struggle faced internally yet profoundly impacting every aspect of our lives. It doesn't manifest as physical bruises or scars but affects our thoughts, emotions, and behaviors. It is a spectrum encompassing moments of overwhelming despair and subtle disquiet that quietly erodes our well-being.

For many, acknowledging mental health struggles feels like admitting defeat. Yet, in truth, recognizing these struggles is the first courageous step toward healing. Mental health issues are not a sign of weakness but an indicator of being human in a complex, demanding world. Stress, anxiety, and depression are often the body's way of signaling that we need to pause, reassess, and realign with our true selves.

Healing begins with understanding. The mind, like the body, has an extraordinary ability to heal when nurtured and cared for. Creating a safe space—whether through therapy, self-reflection, or connecting with others—opens the door to self-compassion and healing. Mental health is not a destination; it is a continuous journey of maintaining balance, resilience, and growth.

**The Connection Between Resilience and Mental Health**

Resilience and mental health are inextricably linked, each reinforcing the other. When our mental health suffers, resilience wanes, making us vulnerable to life's challenges. Conversely, when we cultivate resilience, we strengthen our capacity to maintain mental well-being, even in turbulent times.

Resilience does not eliminate the darkness, but it helps us navigate through it. A resilient mind doesn't deny pain; it embraces it, learning from the experience while seeking the light on the horizon. For instance, moments of profound grief or failure can feel unbearable. Yet, through resilience, we can uncover hidden strengths, gradually rebuilding our lives with newfound wisdom and purpose.

By focusing on positive mental health practices, we can proactively build resilience. Strategies like mindfulness, gratitude, and establishing a support system are more than just coping mechanisms—they're transformative tools that equip us to thrive amid adversity. These practices serve as reminders that while the storm may rage, we have the power to find calm within.

**Prioritizing Mental Health**

Maintaining positive mental health is not just about addressing issues when they arise; it's about taking proactive steps to foster emotional and psychological well-being on a consistent basis. Just as we engage in regular physical exercise to keep our bodies strong and healthy, our minds also need care and attention to thrive. This involves building

habits and routines that nurture mental resilience and emotional balance.

A crucial component of this approach is creating a personalized "mental health toolkit." This toolkit comprises strategies and activities tailored to your unique needs and preferences, ensuring you have resources to draw upon when challenges emerge. The goal is to build a foundation of well-being that prepares you to navigate life's uncertainties with strength and optimism.

**Essential Tools for Your Mental Health Toolkit**

**1. Daily Gratitude Journals**

Gratitude journaling is a simple yet powerful practice. Each day, write down three things you're thankful for—whether they're big or small. It could be as profound as overcoming a personal challenge or as simple as enjoying a good cup of coffee. This practice rewires your brain to focus on the positive aspects of your life, shifting your perspective from scarcity to abundance. Over time, gratitude journaling fosters a sense of contentment and helps counteract the negativity bias that often dominates our thoughts.

**2. Connection Breaks**

In our increasingly digital and fast-paced world, genuine human connection often takes a backseat. Make it a priority to set aside time for meaningful conversations with family, friends, or trusted mentors. Whether it's a phone call, a coffee meetup, or even a walk with a close friend, these moments combat isolation and

remind you that you're not alone. Connection breaks also offer an opportunity to share thoughts and feelings, gain new perspectives, and strengthen your emotional support network.

### 3. Movement and Nature

Physical activity and exposure to nature are two of the most effective ways to rejuvenate the mind. Exercise releases endorphins, the body's natural mood elevators, while nature provides a calming environment that reduces stress and enhances creativity. Combining the two—such as going for a hike, a walk in the park, or a yoga session outdoors—amplifies their benefits. These activities not only improve your physical health but also offer a mental reset, helping you process emotions and return to tasks with renewed clarity.

### 4. Creative Outlets

Creativity isn't just for artists; it's for anyone seeking a meaningful way to express themselves. Engaging in hobbies like painting, writing, cooking, gardening, or playing a musical instrument allows you to channel your emotions constructively. Creative activities provide a sense of accomplishment and joy, reminding you of your ability to create beauty and meaning even in challenging times.

By integrating these practices into your daily routine, you not only enhance your mental health but also strengthen your resilience. This creates a virtuous cycle: improved mental well-being reinforces resilience and resilience, in turn, helps maintain mental health, equipping you to navigate life's ups and downs with greater ease and confidence.

## The Dark Side and the Bright Side

Life's darker moments can feel like an unending void, an oppressive weight that saps our energy and clouds our vision. These periods often arise from heartbreak, the loss of loved ones, or the gnawing pain of unfulfilled expectations and dreams. There are times when uncertainty looms large, and the path forward seems obscured by fog. Yet, within this darkness lies a hidden potential—a transformative power that compels us to confront our vulnerabilities and tap into reserves of inner strength we didn't know we possessed.

Darkness, paradoxically, is both an adversary and a teacher. While the experience of pain, grief, or despair can feel isolating, it also offers an opportunity to delve deep into our inner selves. By facing the discomfort head-on, we uncover truths about who we are and what we value most. These moments strip away superficialities, forcing us to evaluate our priorities and reimagine our path forward.

Embracing the darkness begins with acceptance. It's essential to give ourselves permission to feel—without judgment or shame. It's okay to grieve, to feel anger, sadness, confusion, or even apathy. These emotions are not weaknesses; they are evidence of our humanity. They remind us that we are alive and capable of growth. Resilience is not about bypassing these feelings but rather about sitting with them, allowing them to flow through us. Over time, this practice of acceptance transforms discomfort into clarity, helping us gain profound insights that guide us toward healing and renewal.

## Finding the Light

The bright side of life is not about the absence of challenges—it's about cultivating the ability to find joy, meaning, and purpose in their midst. It's about recognizing that even amidst chaos, there are moments of calm, beauty, and connection that make life worthwhile. The light is found in small, everyday victories: a kind word from a friend, the warmth of the sun on your face, or the satisfaction of overcoming a personal challenge. These moments remind us of the richness and complexity of the human experience.

Resilience plays a crucial role in uncovering the light. It transforms how we view the world, enabling us to see beauty in imperfection and growth in adversity. This shift in perspective doesn't negate the reality of pain but reframes it within a larger narrative of perseverance and transformation. Through resilience, we learn to see challenges not as insurmountable obstacles but as opportunities for personal evolution.

One powerful tool for finding the light is cultivating gratitude. Gratitude helps shift our focus from what we lack to what we already have. When we consciously celebrate even the smallest achievements or joys, we create a sense of abundance that counteracts feelings of scarcity and despair. For example, acknowledging the strength it took to get out of bed on a difficult day or appreciating the support of a loved one reinforces positivity and builds momentum for further growth.

Moreover, finding the light encourages us to develop a sense of purpose. This purpose might stem from helping others, pursuing a

passion, or striving to become the best version of ourselves. Purpose provides an anchor, a reason to keep moving forward even when the road gets tough. When we align our actions with our deeper values, life's challenges become stepping stones rather than stumbling blocks.

## The Dynamic Balance Between Darkness and Light

Understanding the interplay between darkness and light is essential for resilience. Both are integral parts of the human experience. The darkness teaches us to be introspective and to confront what lies beneath the surface. The light, on the other hand, teaches us to celebrate life and cherish its fleeting moments of beauty. Together, they create a dynamic balance that shapes our journey and enables us to grow into more compassionate, self-aware individuals.

Through resilience, we learn to navigate the spectrum of emotions, finding strength in vulnerability and joy in perseverance. Each moment of darkness is an opportunity to discover our capacity for light, and each moment of light reminds us of the strength we gained from enduring the darkness. This balance is what makes life meaningful, complex, and deeply rewarding.

## Special Notes: Rewiring Thought Patterns

Our thoughts shape our reality. Negative thought patterns can trap us in cycles of self-doubt and despair, while positive thinking fosters resilience and hope. The process of rewiring these patterns begins with awareness. By identifying limiting beliefs and reframing them, we create space for growth and self-compassion.

For example, instead of thinking, "I'm not strong enough," reframe it to, "I'm learning and growing stronger every day." This simple shift changes how we perceive challenges, transforming them from obstacles into opportunities.

### 7. Tools for Healing

| Tool | Activity | Benefit |
|---|---|---|
| Guided Meditation | Use apps or recordings for daily meditative practices. | Reduces stress and enhances emotional balance. |
| Cognitive Behavioral Techniques | Challenge negative thoughts and replace them with constructive ones. | Builds a healthier, more resilient mindset. |
| Support Groups | Join communities focused on shared experiences. | Provides connection and reduces isolation. |
| Nature Therapy | Spend time outdoors, observing and reflecting. | Boosts mood and fosters creativity. |

### Filling the Mind With Resilience

Resilience is a skill that grows with practice. By consistently integrating positive habits into our lives, we create a mental reservoir of strength and hope. This reservoir enables us to face future challenges with confidence, knowing that we have the tools to overcome them.

*"We are not defined by our wounds but by the strength we show in healing them."*

This chapter has taught us that healing is a journey, not a destination. It begins with acknowledging the darkness and actively seeking the light. Through the integration of practical tools, proactive mental

health care, and a resilient mindset, we can transform our wounds into wisdom. Life's challenges may leave scars, but those scars are testaments to our strength and capacity for growth. By nurturing our mental well-being, we equip ourselves to embrace the fullness of life with courage and optimism.

*"Healing doesn't mean the damage never existed. It means the damage no longer controls our lives." – Unknown.*

# Chapter 7:

# Outcome Through

# Self-Redemption

*"The struggle you're in today is developing the strength you need for tomorrow."*— Robert Tew

This powerful quote serves that every struggle, no matter how difficult, is a vital part of our journey.

Resilience is the cornerstone of personal growth and transformation. It is the ability to rise above life's challenges, learn from setbacks, and persist in the pursuit of your goals, regardless of the obstacles in your path. Self-redemption, on the other hand, is the process of forgiving oneself for past mistakes, making amends, and becoming a better version of oneself in the aftermath. Together, resilience and self-redemption create a powerful combination for healing and transformation, allowing individuals to reclaim their strength and purpose.

Every story has a turning point. That pivotal moment when a character, having been worn down by life's trials, finds within themselves the resilience to rise above adversity. It is here, in the face of challenge, where the raw power of human strength is forged. The stories we remember—the ones that ignite something inside us—are those that show us how resilience is not just an abstract idea, but a

transformative force, shaping lives and outcomes. The narrative of triumph over hardship isn't always easy, but it is necessary.

This chapter explores how resilience, depicted in countless stories across cultures and histories, serves as an invaluable source of inspiration for those facing adversity. Resilience is not an innate trait, but a cultivated strength that is developed through facing challenges, learning from failure, and continually striving toward a more empowered version of oneself.

This section will explore a series of tools that can help you build resilience, foster self-redemption, and strengthen your emotional and mental well-being. Each tool is backed by actionable steps, practical advice, and real-life examples of how individuals have applied them to overcome personal struggles. By incorporating these tools into your daily life, you can develop a deeper sense of inner strength, confidence, and a renewed sense of purpose.

Through both practical tools and philosophical insights, we examine the deeper layers of resilience and its transformative power in reshaping not only our circumstances but also our own self-worth. The key message of this chapter is simple yet profound: **Resilience is not the absence of hardship, but the ability to emerge from it with greater wisdom, strength, and a renewed sense of purpose.**

Resilience is the heartbeat of every struggle, the thread that ties failure to success. It is not simply the ability to endure, but the courage to face difficult circumstances and continue moving forward. In our stories, both fictional and real, we see resilience take on many forms.

It can be found in the unsung heroes who push past doubt, in the moments of introspection where a person realizes that redemption isn't just a distant hope, but a near and achievable reality.

But resilience is not something that happens by chance. It is a theme deliberately woven into the tapestry of every powerful narrative. Whether it's the classic hero's journey or a more modern retelling, the characters we admire most are often those who face their struggles with unwavering perseverance. And it is through their resilience that they find redemption—not in a world that always supports them, but in a world that challenges them to grow. Their stories show us that success does not come from avoiding difficulty but from facing it head-on with determination, courage, and a willingness to change.

Consider the protagonist who picks themselves up after a catastrophic failure and keeps moving forward. This is not a passive act of waiting for things to improve. No, it is an active choice to keep moving, to believe that the journey holds more than just pain but also possibility. These stories compel us to ask: What would be uncertain if we decided, just like them, to embrace the challenge, even when the outcome is uncertain?

The choice to move through adversity reveals the true nature of resilience. Often, our doubts and fears feel louder than our desires for success. We hear them—whispering, taunting, questioning our every step. But those who overcome find a way to drown out the noise. They realize that resilience isn't about denying those doubts; it's about recognizing that they are only temporary, while the will to rise is permanent.

One of the most poignant aspects of resilience in storytelling is the idea of self-redemption. After all, redemption is not given from the outside; it is earned through transformation. Having been tested and broken, a person learns how to put the pieces back together in a new way. They discover parts of themselves they didn't know existed: strength, courage, and wisdom they never thought they could have. The hero who stumbles and falls but still chooses to rise is, in fact, the one who has already won. In their journey, they embody the very essence of resilience—a determination to shape their own outcome, no matter how steep the climb.

**The Power of Resilience in Stories and Life**

In every corner of the world, resilience is the thread that binds remarkable stories of triumph. Think of characters like Nelson Mandela, who overcame nearly three decades of imprisonment, or the mythological heroes who, after falling into despair, rise again, learning invaluable lessons along the way. These stories resonate because they showcase the ultimate human truth: challenges are inevitable, but how we respond to them defines us.

Resilience has been the backbone of some of the most powerful stories ever told stories that resonate deeply because they reflect the universal human experience of struggle, hope, and eventual triumph. From the ancient myth of Hercules' Twelve Labors to modern biographies like Maya Angelou's *I Know Why the Caged Bird Sings*, stories of resilience have always carried a powerful message: despite the overwhelming odds, the human spirit can overcome great challenges.

One powerful lesson embedded in these stories is that resilience is not about avoiding pain or avoiding difficulties—rather, it is about how we respond to those difficulties. In many of these stories, heroes are not born with inherent power; they grow stronger through adversity, often learning their most profound lessons through failure, loss, and hardship. These stories remind us that resilience doesn't just restore us after trauma—it transforms us, shaping us into more capable versions of ourselves.

In the real world, resilience operates in much the same way. It's easy to believe that those who succeed or achieve greatness are somehow immune to hardship, but in truth, they have simply learned how to use adversity as a tool for growth. Resilience is built on perseverance, a mindset that refuses to accept defeat, and the unwavering belief that every setback is an opportunity for a comeback.

Resilience is a quality cultivated not in moments of calm but during the storm. It is found in the grit to keep moving forward when circumstances seem insurmountable. From literature to real life, resilient individuals are those who choose to face their struggles head-on, adapt, and emerge stronger. This chapter draws parallels between these timeless narratives and the practical steps everyone can take to build their own resilience.

In the stories we tell, resilience is often depicted not as an inherent trait, but as a learned ability. Characters who fail are given the opportunity to try again, to fall and get up, and with each failure, they grow. This is the heartbeat of self-redemption—an understanding that even the darkest moments can be the birthplace of something greater. Through resilience, they learn to navigate the shadows of their past and shape their own future.

## Resilience as a Tool for Self-Redemption

Self-redemption is the act of reclaiming your sense of worth and potential, even when the world or your own actions have led you astray. It's a deeply personal journey that calls for radical self-compassion, honesty, and a firm belief in the possibility of change. Stories of self-redemption are woven into our cultural fabric, from classic literature to modern films, illustrating the notion that Self-redemption is one of the most potent expressions of resilience. It is the process of reclaiming one's worth and potential, especially when we've made mistakes or feel disconnected from our true selves. Self-redemption is a deeply human pursuit, and it is intricately tied to the resilience that allows us to rise above our past and redefine our future.

Consider the story of Viktor Frankl, a neurologist and psychiatrist who survived the Holocaust. In his book *Man's Search for Meaning*, Frankl writes about how even in the most dire circumstances, people who were able to find meaning in their suffering were able to survive and even thrive. For Frankl, this is the ultimate power of self-redemption: the ability to find meaning and purpose even in the most dehumanizing and challenging of situations.

Similarly, many individuals experience self-redemption not through grand, public acts, but through quieter, more personal transformations. It's the person who acknowledges their mistakes, learns from them, and takes responsibility for their actions. It's the individual who, after facing failure or loss, picks themselves up and moves forward with a renewed sense of purpose. In each case, resilience is the key factor that

allows us to transcend our limitations and find new, empowering ways to engage with the world.

Through resilience, self-redemption is not about forgetting our past or pretending it didn't happen. It is about learning to accept our flaws and failures, embracing the lessons they impart, and using them to grow. It's a process that requires self-compassion, honesty, and courage—the courage to believe that we are always capable of reinvention, no matter how far we may have fallen or how many times we may have stumbled.

.Just as the stories of heroes remind us that redemption is possible, so too can we use our own narratives as tools for growth. By embracing failure, learning from it, and understanding that setbacks are not the end but part of the journey, we open ourselves up to a powerful process of self-redemption.

**Practical Tools for Building Resilience and Achieving Self-Redemption**

In the journey of resilience, it's crucial to have practical tools that support and guide your efforts. Tools don't just provide structure—they create a routine, a rhythm that makes resilience a habit, not just a reactive response to crisis. The tools presented here are designed to help you understand your own resilience, track your progress, and equip you with strategies to keep going, no matter what challenges arise.

*These tools are rooted in psychological principles and are aimed at nurturing not only your ability to endure but to thrive. They will help you shift your perspective on setbacks, recognize growth even in moments of struggle, and ultimately create a life built on inner strength and perseverance:*

**Key Tools for Cultivating Resilience:**

1.  **The Reflection Journal:** Self-reflection is one of the most effective tools for building resilience. By regularly documenting challenges, emotional responses, and growth, you engage in an active process of self-awareness. This helps you identify patterns in your responses to difficulty, giving you insights into how to handle future obstacles. By revisiting your journal entries, you gain the perspective of time— seeing how far you've come despite hardships. This process turns your struggles into a personal narrative of growth, reinforcing your ability to overcome future challenges.

2.  **The Growth Mindset Mantra:** A resilient mindset is rooted in the belief that we can improve, change, and learn from our challenges. The growth mindset mantra is a tool that helps you reframe obstacles as opportunities. By repeating affirmations like "I am capable of growth" or "Challenges strengthen me," you cultivate an internal dialogue that nurtures perseverance. This tool encourages you to see setbacks as part of your evolution, reminding you that your abilities and potential are not fixed but can always be expanded through effort and learning.

3. **The Failure Reframe:** Failure is one of the most powerful catalysts for growth, but only if we choose to see it that way. The Failure Reframe tool is about transforming your perception of failure. When you fail, instead of falling into despair, ask yourself: "What can I learn from this?" "How will this experience make me better?" By writing down the lessons from each failure and setting new, adjusted goals, you break free from the cycle of self-doubt and move forward stronger and wiser.

4. **The Goal Breakdown Chart:** Large goals can often feel overwhelming, leading to procrastination and paralysis. The Goal Breakdown Chart takes the enormity of your goals and breaks them into small, manageable steps. Each step is like a mini-victory, providing you with a sense of accomplishment and momentum. This process reduces feelings of overwhelm, helping you stay focused and proactive as you work toward larger objectives.

5. **Resilience Reminders Board:** A visual cue for resilience, the Resilience Reminders Board is a space where you collect images, quotes, and affirmations that inspire strength. When you are facing difficult times, having these reminders in your environment can serve as a powerful signal that you are capable of overcoming whatever comes your way. This tool ensures that resilience becomes part of your daily environment, rather than just a concept you think about in times of crisis.

6. **Support Circle Map:** Resilience thrives when it is supported by a network of encouragement and assistance. The Support Circle

Map helps you identify your network of supportive people—friends, mentors, family members, and even communities that offer guidance. Knowing who you can turn to during challenging times makes you feel less isolated and provides a crucial source of emotional strength. Resilience is never about-facing difficulties alone; it's about knowing when to reach out for help.

7. **Progress Tracker:** It's easy to feel like you're not making progress, especially when things seem difficult. A Progress Tracker helps you track even the smallest steps forward, which can provide a sense of accomplishment and motivate you to continue. By celebrating milestones—whether it's completing a task or overcoming a minor setback—you affirm that resilience is built one step at a time.

8. **The "Why" Compass:** Knowing your core purpose is essential to staying resilient. The "Why" Compass helps you reconnect with your fundamental reasons for pursuing a goal, especially when the going gets tough. Revisiting your "why" when you're discouraged helps you stay focused on the bigger picture, reminding you that your struggle is part of a larger purpose.

9. **Mindfulness Reset Timer:** Resilience requires emotional regulation, which is supported by mindfulness. The Mindfulness Reset Timer is a tool that prompts you to pause, breathe, and reset in moments of stress. Just a few minutes of focused breathing or grounding exercises can help you regain clarity, reduce anxiety, and approach challenges with a more balanced perspective.

**10. Self-Compassion Letter:** Self-compassion is a cornerstone of resilience. The Self-Compassion Letter encourages you to treat yourself with the same kindness and understanding you would offer a loved one. By writing a letter to yourself after a setback, you acknowledge your struggles and encourage healing. This practice reduces self-criticism and nurtures emotional well-being, providing a foundation for ongoing growth and redemption.

**Hypothetical Examples of Applying the Tools for Building Resilience and Self-Redemption**

**1. The Reflection Journal**

**Examples:**

**Maria**, a small business owner, faced several obstacles during the first few years of her venture. She struggled with cash flow issues and the pressure of balancing her business with personal life. To manage her feelings and track her growth, Maria started using a **Reflection Journal**. Every evening, she wrote about the challenges she faced that day, focusing on what worked, what didn't, and what lessons she could apply moving forward. Re-reading her journal over the months, Maria noticed her resilience growing. She was no longer overwhelmed by challenges but instead found ways to turn each obstacle into a learning experience. Over time, she used her journal not just as a log of events, but as a way to reconnect with her purpose and motivations.

- **Purpose:** To track emotional responses and progress, helping her find growth even in difficult times.

- **Steps to Take:** Maria wrote daily or weekly entries about her challenges and progress, revisiting them to track her growth.

- **Benefit:** Enhanced self-awareness, clarity on progress, and the recognition of how she evolved over time.

## The Reflection Journal –Overcoming Job Loss

**Sarah** recently lost her job after working in the same position for over 10 years. She felt devastated and unsure of what her next step should be. To process her emotions and rebuild her resilience, Sarah started using **The Reflection Journal**. Every evening, she wrote about her feelings of disappointment, but also focused on the lessons she was learning about herself, her strengths, and her career goals. She started noticing patterns in her reflections—particularly, that she thrived when she was allowed to take on new challenges and grow. Revisiting these entries regularly, Sarah realized how much she had grown in the face of adversity. Over time, her journal helped her stay grounded, leading her to pursue a new career path she had never considered before, one that aligned better with her passions.

- **Purpose:** Sarah used journaling to track emotional responses and reflect on personal growth.

- **Steps to Take:** She wrote about her struggles and revisited her journal entries to track her progress.

- **Benefit:** The journal enhanced Sarah's self-awareness, helped her process emotions, and made her see her journey from a perspective of growth.

## 2. The Growth Mindset Mantra

**Example**:

**David**, a young professional in a competitive marketing firm, faced frequent setbacks in his projects, which led to a loss of confidence. Realizing that his negative thinking was holding him back, David started using the **Growth Mindset Mantra** by repeating affirmations like, "I am capable of learning from my mistakes," and "Every challenge is an opportunity to improve." Every morning before work, he took a few minutes to center himself with these affirmations. Slowly, he started to view setbacks as necessary steps toward improvement rather than failures. This shift in mindset boosted his self-confidence and eventually led to his promotion within the company.

- **Purpose:** To build resilience by reinforcing the idea that skills and abilities grow with effort.

- **Steps to Take:** David created a list of empowering affirmations and repeated them every day, particularly during challenging moments.

- **Benefit:** Increased self-confidence, a more positive outlook, and a continual drive for self-improvement.

## 2. The Growth Mindset Mantra – John's Commitment to Physical Fitness

John had always struggled with his physical health, and after a few failed attempts to lose weight, he felt discouraged. He decided to adopt **The Growth Mindset Mantra** by repeating affirmations like

"I am capable of growth," and "Challenges help me grow stronger," every morning and before workouts. Initially, John wasn't seeing immediate results, but by continuing to tell himself that his efforts were contributing to his long-term success, he began to shift his mindset. His confidence grew, and he gradually found the discipline to push through tough workout sessions. Slowly, he started noticing improvements in his strength, stamina, and overall well-being, which reaffirmed his belief in his ability to improve through effort.

- **Purpose**: John used affirmations to help him believe in his ability to grow and improve.

- **Steps to Take**: He repeated positive affirmations every day and particularly during moments of doubt or struggle.

- **Benefit**: The mantra helped John develop a more positive outlook, boosting his confidence and promoting continuous progress in his fitness journey.

## 3. The Failure Reframe

**Example:**

**Jessica**, a recent graduate, applied for several jobs in her field but faced rejection after rejection. Each rejection was disheartening, and she began doubting her abilities. Instead of letting the rejections define her, Jessica used **The Failure Reframe** technique. After each rejection, she would write down what went wrong, what she could learn from the experience, and how she would adjust her approach moving forward. This allowed her to treat each rejection as a stepping stone rather than a setback. Over time, her confidence grew, and her

resume became more polished. Eventually, Jessica landed her dream job because she embraced learning from each failure.

- **Purpose:** To reframe setbacks as opportunities for growth.

- **Steps to Take:** After each rejection, Jessica would reflect on her actions, learn from them, and adapt for future applications.

- **Benefit:** Reduced fear of failure, better learning from experiences, and the cultivation of a growth mindset.

### 3. The Failure Reframe – Emily's Career Setback

Emily worked for a tech company for several years, but after a major project failed, she was on the verge of giving up. Instead of letting the failure define her, Emily used **The Failure Reframe** to view the setback as an opportunity to learn. She wrote down what went wrong, acknowledged where she could have done better, and focused on the skills and lessons she had gained throughout the experience. Emily realized that failure wasn't an endpoint but a chance to grow. By reframing her failure, she developed a more resilient attitude and started applying for higher-level positions, ultimately landing her dream job at another company.

- **Purpose:** Emily transformed her failure into a learning experience.

- **Steps to Take:** After the setback, she reflected on what went wrong, identified the lessons learned, and strategized how to improve moving forward.

- **Benefit:** The failure reframe helped Emily overcome fear, build a growth mindset, and turn setbacks into valuable stepping stones for future success.

## 4. Goal Breakdown Chart

**Example:**

**Leo**, an aspiring author, wanted to write a novel but was overwhelmed by the size of the task. Instead of feeling paralyzed, Leo used a **Goal Breakdown Chart**. He wrote down his ultimate goal of completing a novel and then broke it down into manageable steps—first, researching for a month, then writing a chapter outline, then drafting 500 words a day. Each step was assigned a weekly target. By focusing on one small task at a time, Leo didn't feel overwhelmed. After a year, he completed his novel by continually working on smaller, bite-sized tasks.

- **Purpose:** To reduce overwhelm and create a clear, actionable path to achieving long-term goals.

- **Steps to Take:** Leo divided his large goal into smaller tasks, focused on one task at a time, and reevaluated his progress weekly.

- **Benefit:** Increased focus, productivity, and a clear path to achievement.

## 5. Goal Breakdown Chart

### Michael's Long-Term Entrepreneurial Dream

Michael dreamed of starting his own business, but the idea felt overwhelming. He knew it was a huge undertaking, but he was unsure of where to begin. Using **The Goal Breakdown Chart**, he divided his business goal into smaller, more manageable steps. Each week, he focused on one task—researching his target market, creating a business plan, securing funding, and building his website. By breaking down the process,

Michael was able to focus on one task at a time, reducing his anxiety and ensuring steady progress toward his goal. Over the course of a year, his small steps added up, and he successfully launched his business.

- **Purpose:** Michael used the chart to break down a large goal into actionable steps.

- **Steps to Take:** He identified his ultimate goal, divided it into smaller tasks, and worked on them weekly.

- **Benefit:** The chart kept Michael focused, reducing overwhelm and providing a clear path toward achieving his long-term vision.

### 5. Resilience Reminders Board

**Example:**

**Sophia**, after going through a difficult divorce, found herself struggling with motivation. To help herself stay grounded during challenging moments, she created a **Resilience Reminders Board** in her living room. On the board, she placed quotes like "You are stronger than you think," photos of happier times with her children, and affirmations such as "This too shall pass." When she felt particularly low, Sophia would glance at the board, and the visual cues would give her the strength to keep moving forward. Eventually, she felt empowered and began focusing on the positive aspects of her life, such as her children and career.

- **Purpose:** To provide ongoing visual reminders that inspire resilience and positivity.

- **Steps to Take:** Sophia created a reminder board with motivating visuals and placed it in a frequently visited area.

- **Benefit:** Kept her motivated and inspired, reinforcing positive thinking when needed most.

## 5. Resilience Reminders Board – Clara's Post-Divorce Healing

Clara went through a difficult divorce that left her emotionally drained. She found it hard to stay positive in the face of her pain, so she created a **Resilience Reminders Board** to help her stay motivated and inspired. She filled the board with affirmations like "You are strong," images of happy memories with her children, and quotes that encouraged perseverance. Whenever Clara felt discouraged, she would look at the board, which helped her remember her inner strength. Over time, the visual reminders on the board kept her motivated and allowed her to heal more quickly.

- **Purpose:** Clara used the board to keep herself motivated and reminded of her strength.
- **Steps to Take:** She created a visual reminder board with affirmations and personal milestones, placing it in a visible location.
- **Benefit:** The board provided constant encouragement and helped Clara reinforce positive thinking, keeping her focused on healing.

## 6. Support Circle Map

**Example:**

**Tom**, a recovering addict, often felt isolated and unsure of how to continue his journey toward sobriety. To create a sense of community, Tom made a **Support Circle Map**, listing all the people and resources

he could turn to for help—his sponsor, his close friends, his family, and a local support group. This map helped him visualize the people who cared about him and could provide support when he needed it. Whenever Tom felt tempted or discouraged, he would reach out to someone on his map, receiving the encouragement he needed to stay strong.

- **Purpose:** To map out supportive relationships and resources, ensuring that help is always within reach.

- **Steps to Take:** Tom identified and connected with his network regularly, reaching out for support when needed.

- **Benefit:** Created a strong support network that kept Tom accountable, reducing feelings of isolation and improving his resilience.

### 6. Support Circle Map – Kevin's Recovery from Addiction

Kevin struggled with addiction for several years and often felt isolated. He created a **Support Circle Map** to identify the people who had supported him during his recovery journey, such as his family, friends, and support groups. The map helped Kevin visualize who he could turn to in moments of weakness or self-doubt. By regularly reaching out to his support circle, he felt more connected and less alone. As a result, Kevin was able to stay committed to his recovery and gradually rebuild his life.

- **Purpose:** Kevin used the map to visualize and organize his support network.

- **Steps to Take:** He mapped out his supportive relationships and regularly engaged with his circle for encouragement and advice.

- **Benefit:** The support circle map strengthened Kevin's sense of community and empowered him to seek help when needed, improving his resilience.

## 7. Progress Tracker

**Example:**

**Olivia**, an entrepreneur, decided to start a podcast but felt overwhelmed by the scope of the project. She created a **Progress Tracker** to help monitor her daily actions and small victories. Each day, Olivia tracked specific goals, such as writing episode scripts, scheduling interviews, or recording episodes. When she felt discouraged, she reviewed her progress tracker, which showed her how far she had come, even in just a few weeks. The tracker gave her a sense of accomplishment and kept her motivated as she saw the fruits of her hard work adding up.

- **Purpose:** To track small wins and ensure consistent progress toward larger goals.

- **Steps to Take:** Olivia tracked her daily progress, reviewing and celebrating small milestones.

- **Benefit:** Increased accountability, a sense of accomplishment, and the maintenance of momentum.

## 8. The "Why" Compass

**Example:**

**Nina**, a single mother working two jobs, often felt exhausted and discouraged. To keep herself motivated, she used **The "Why" Compass**, reminding herself of her core purpose—providing a better life for her children and giving them the opportunities she never had. On particularly tough days, she would write down her "why" on a piece of paper and keep it in her wallet, so she could pull it out whenever she needed a reminder. This helped Nina reconnect with her core purpose and reminded her that the sacrifices she made were for a greater good.

- **Purpose:** To reconnect with one's core motivations during difficult times.

- **Steps to Take:** Nina wrote down her "why" and revisited it when she faced challenges.

- **Benefit:** Reignited passion and motivation, helping her stay focused on her long-term vision.

## 9. Mindfulness Reset Timer

**Example:**

**Ethan**, a corporate lawyer, often found himself overwhelmed by stress during long hours at the office. To manage his stress, he set a **Mindfulness Reset Timer** for five-minute breaks throughout the day. During these breaks, he would step away from his desk, close his eyes, and focus on his breathing. These short mindfulness sessions helped him stay calm, improve his focus, and reduce stress. As a result, Ethan found he could be more productive and maintain a better work-life balance.

- **Purpose:** To practice mindfulness, reduce stress, and stay grounded in the present moment.

- **Steps to Take:** Ethan set a timer for short mindfulness sessions throughout the day, focusing on his breath to reset his mental state.

- **Benefit:** Reduced stress, improved focus, and better emotional regulation.

## 10. Self-Compassion Letter

**Example:**

**Lily**, a college student, was struggling with feelings of inadequacy after receiving a disappointing grade on an important exam. She used **The Self-Compassion Letter** tool to write a letter to herself, acknowledging the pain and disappointment she was feeling but also offering herself kindness and encouragement. In the letter, Lily wrote about how she had worked hard and was capable of learning from the experience. Reading the letter brought her comfort, and she found the strength to move forward with a renewed sense of self-love and determination.

- **Purpose:** To foster self-compassion during difficult times, helping to counter self-criticism and promote emotional healing.

- **Steps to Take:** Lily wrote herself a letter of understanding and compassion, then read it whenever she needed emotional comfort.

- **Benefit:** Encouraged self-acceptance, reduced self-criticism, and supported emotional healing and resilience.

66

**Final Thoughts**

Each of these examples demonstrates how these tools can be integrated into everyday life to build resilience, self-redemption, and a sense of empowerment. Whether you are struggling with personal setbacks, professional challenges, or emotional hurdles, these tools provide practical, actionable strategies to help you stay strong and grow through adversity.

These hypothetical examples show how applying these resilience tools in real life can transform adversity into opportunity for personal growth. Each individual faced a challenge that required resilience, self-reflection, and action. By implementing the strategies outlined in this chapter, they were able to break through limitations, embrace failure, and take actionable steps toward building a stronger, more empowered version of themselves. Whether you're in the midst of a difficult career transition like Sarah, struggling with self-doubt like John, or facing major life changes like Clara, these tools provide a practical roadmap for overcoming obstacles and shaping a resilient, self-redeemed future.

Each of these examples demonstrates how these tools can be integrated into everyday life to build resilience, self-redemption, and a sense of empowerment. Whether you are struggling with personal setbacks, professional challenges, or emotional hurdles, these tools provide practical, actionable strategies to help you stay strong and grow through adversity.

## A Strategy for Implementation

While these tools are powerful on their own, the key to building lasting resilience lies in how you implement them. To integrate these practices into your daily life, follow this step-by-step approach:

1. **Start Small and Be Consistent:** Begin by selecting a few tools that resonate with you the most. You don't need to use all of them at once. By starting small, you create manageable habits that become easier to integrate into your life. Consistency is more important than intensity—small daily actions will have a cumulative effect over time.

2. **Create a Routine:** Building resilience requires routine. Set aside time each day or week for these practices. Whether it's journaling every morning, reviewing your goals every Sunday, or using your Mindfulness Reset Timer throughout the day, incorporating these tools into a routine helps make them habitual.

3. **Track Your Progress and Reflect Regularly:** Regular reflection is key to building resilience. Set aside time to evaluate your progress—how far have you come? What challenges have you overcome? What have you learned? This reflective process helps you appreciate your growth and identify areas for improvement.

4. **Celebrate Milestones, No Matter How Small:** Every victory, no matter how minor, is a step forward. Celebrate your progress—whether it's sticking to your goal breakdown plan, showing up for yourself emotionally, or simply getting through a tough week. Acknowledging these small wins helps to sustain motivation and reinforces the positive habits you're building.

## The Power of Perspective

The first step in shaping the outcome of your struggles is changing the way you view them. Instead of perceiving challenges as insurmountable hurdles, try reframing them as opportunities for growth. This shift in perspective is powerful—it allows you to see adversity not as something to be avoided but as a necessary part of your development.

A prime example of this shift in perspective is the story of *Rachel*, a young woman who struggled with self-esteem issues after failing multiple job interviews. She had been conditioned to view failure as a personal deficiency. However, by embracing a growth mindset, she was able to reframe her failures as learning experiences. She asked herself, "What can I learn from this? How can I improve next time?" This change in mindset not only helped her recover but ultimately led to her landing a job that was a perfect fit for her skills and aspirations.

## Tool 1: The Growth Mindset Mantra

A Growth Mindset Mantra can be instrumental in reshaping how we approach setbacks. By affirming daily that challenges are an opportunity to grow, we begin to internalize this mindset.

**Example:** After her third failed interview, Rachel started affirming daily, "I am capable of growth, and every setback makes me stronger." Over time, this mantra rewired her brain, helping her approach challenges with optimism and perseverance.

69

## Tool 2: The Failure Reframe

One of the most common reactions to failure is self-blame and defeat. However, this mindset can leave us stuck in a cycle of shame and discouragement. The Failure Reframe tool allows us to change our perspective on failure and see it as an opportunity for learning and self-improvement.

**Example:** *James*, an aspiring musician, faced constant rejection from record labels. Initially, he took each rejection personally, believing it meant he wasn't good enough. However, when he used the Failure Reframe tool, he began to analyze each setback as a learning opportunity. He reviewed feedback, improved his music, and used rejection to fuel his creativity. Eventually, he signed with a label that recognized his unique sound and determination.*

By reframing failure, James was able to develop a resilience that not only improved his craft but also led him to success. The Failure Reframe empowers you to transform setbacks into opportunities for refinement, growth, and eventual triumph.

## Tool 3: The Support Circle Map

No one is truly alone in their struggles. Having a network of supportive individuals can make all the difference in overcoming adversity. Whether it's family, friends, mentors, or communities, the support we receive helps us feel understood, encouraged, and capable of moving forward.

**Example:** *Emma* was going through a difficult divorce and felt isolated and overwhelmed. When she created her Support Circle Map, she realized that she had a network of friends, family, and colleagues who could offer emotional support. She reached out to her close friend, Sarah, who had gone through a similar experience, and found comfort in their conversations. With Sarah's encouragement, Emma was able to regain her confidence and move forward with a clear sense of purpose.

A Support Circle Map not only provides emotional sustenance but also practical guidance when we are too overwhelmed to make decisions on our own. By identifying who can support us and in what ways, we gain a sense of connection and relief during tough times.

**Tool 4: The Reflection Journal**

A Reflection Journal is an invaluable tool for tracking your emotional journey through struggles and triumphs. By writing about your experiences, challenges, and personal growth, you create a tangible record of how you are shaping your future.

**Example:** *Michael* had struggled with addiction for years. During his recovery, he used a Reflection Journal to document his daily thoughts, feelings, and progress. When he looked back at his early entries, he was amazed at how far he had come. Writing about his struggles helped him process his emotions, stay accountable, and continue working toward his ultimate goal of sobriety.

By dedicating time to reflect on your experiences, you allow yourself to see how far you've come. The Reflection Journal not only helps in

tracking progress but also in identifying patterns and areas for growth, further solidifying your sense of resilience and empowerment.

**Tool 5: The "Why" Compass**

In moments of doubt and discouragement, reconnecting with your "why" can provide the clarity and motivation needed to persevere. The "Why" Compass allows you to articulate your core purpose and revisit it when challenges arise, ensuring that your long-term vision remains intact despite the struggles you face.

**Example:** *Olivia*, an athlete recovering from an injury, faced moments where she questioned whether she would ever regain her strength. During these low points, she revisited her "Why" Compass, reminding herself of her passion for the sport and her desire to inspire others. This reminder helped her maintain focus and work tirelessly through physical therapy, eventually returning to competition stronger than before.

The "Why" Compass serves as an anchor during turbulent times, ensuring that your larger vision helps guide your decisions and actions, no matter the obstacles in your way.

In the end, the stories of resilience are the stories of the human spirit. They remind us that our failures don't define us; it's our ability to rise again that does. We are always given the choice to shape our own outcomes, and through resilience, we can reclaim our path—even in the most challenging times.

> *"Resilience is not about avoiding the storm but learning how to dance in the rain."*— **Anonymous**

While the road to resilience and redemption may be difficult, there are several tools that can help guide you through the process, making each step more intentional and manageable. These tools are designed not only to help you bounce back from adversity but also to ensure that you continue to grow and evolve into the person you're meant to be. Through consistent practice, these tools can shift your perspective, empower your decisions, and enable you to thrive in the face of challenges.

## Table of Tools for Building Resilience and Self-Redemption

The following tools are designed to help you cultivate resilience, foster self-redemption, and build the inner strength necessary to overcome life's challenges. Each tool serves a specific purpose, provides actionable steps for implementation, and offers key benefits that support your growth.

| Tool | Description | How to Use It | Purpose | Steps to Take | Benefits |
|------|-------------|---------------|---------|---------------|----------|
| The Reflection Journal | A dedicated space to reflect on challenges, emotions, and growth. | Write regularly about struggles faced, lessons learned, and personal progress. Revisit past entries to see growth. | To reflect on challenges, track emotional responses, and assess personal growth. | 1. Dedicate time each day or week to write about your challenges. 2. Focus on the lessons learned and any progress made. 3. Revisit past entries regularly to recognize growth. | - Enhances self-awareness - Provides clarity on progress - Helps recognize patterns in your struggles |

| Tool | Description | How to Use It | Purpose | Steps to Take | Benefits |
|---|---|---|---|---|---|
| **The Growth Mindset Mantra** | Affirmations that reinforce the belief that abilities can be developed through effort and perseverance. | Use daily affirmations such as "I am capable of growth" or "Challenges help me grow stronger." Repeat them during tough times. | To cultivate a belief that abilities and strength can be developed through effort and perseverance. | 1. Create a list of positive affirmations (e.g., "I am capable of growth," "Challenges help me grow stronger"). 2. Repeat these affirmations daily, especially when faced with difficulty. | - Promotes a positive outlook - Increases self-confidence - Encourages continuous improvement |
| **The Failure Reframe** | A tool for transforming failures into learning opportunities. | After a setback, write down what went wrong, what you learned, and how you will apply that lesson moving forward. | To transform failure into a learning opportunity and break the cycle of negative thinking. | 1. After a setback, pause and reflect on what went wrong. 2. Identify the lessons learned. 3. Write down how you will use this experience to improve moving forward. | - Reduces fear of failure - Cultivates a growth mindset - Turns setbacks into stepping stones |
| **Goal Breakdown Chart** | A strategy to break down large goals into smaller, actionable steps. | Divide big goals into smaller, achievable tasks. Focus on completing one step at a time. Reevaluate every week. | To break down large, overwhelming goals into smaller, manageable tasks that can be achieved incrementally. | 1. Write down your ultimate goal. 2. Break it down into smaller tasks and assign deadlines. 3. Focus on completing one task at a time. Reevaluate weekly. | - Increases focus and productivity - Reduces overwhelm - Provides a clear path toward achievement |

| Tool | Description | How to Use It | Purpose | Steps to Take | Benefits |
|---|---|---|---|---|---|
| **Resilience Reminders Board** | A visual board with quotes, images, and personal reminders that inspire resilience. | Place it somewhere visible. Include motivational quotes, personal milestones, or images that remind you of your strength. | To keep motivating reminders visible that reinforce strength and resilience during tough moments. | 1. Create a board with quotes, pictures, or affirmations. 2. Place it in a space you see daily (e.g., your workspace or bedroom). 3. Revisit it when you feel discouraged. | - Keeps you inspired and motivated - Acts as a visual cue for resilience - Reinforces positive thinking |
| **Support Circle Map** | A visual map that outlines your network of supportive people and resources. | Identify friends, family, mentors, or communities that offer encouragement and assistance. Reach out when needed. | To identify and map out your network of supportive people and resources who can help you stay resilient. | 1. List people who offer encouragement, help, or support (e.g., friends, family, mentors). 2. Identify who to reach out to in different situations (emotional support, advice, etc.). 3. Regularly connect with your support circle. | - Builds a solid support network - Encourages reaching out for help when needed - Fosters a sense of belonging |
| **Progress Tracker** | A tool to monitor daily or weekly progress toward resilience-building goals. | Use a journal or digital tracker to note small wins and incremental steps. Celebrate each milestone along the way. | To monitor daily or weekly progress towards goals, ensuring consistent movement towards personal growth. | 1. Record specific actions or milestones you want to track. 2. Review and update the tracker regularly. 3. Celebrate small victories along the way. | - Provides accountability - Creates a sense of accomplishment - Keeps momentum going |

| Tool | Description | How to Use It | Purpose | Steps to Take | Benefits |
|---|---|---|---|---|---|
| The "Why" Compass | A tool to reconnect with your core purpose when facing a tough challenge. | Write down your purpose or motivating reason for overcoming struggles. Revisit this when you feel discouraged. | To reconnect with your core purpose, especially when feeling discouraged or lost during difficult times. | 1. Write down your core purpose or the reason you are working toward your goals. 2. Revisit this "why" when facing obstacles. 3. Use it as a touchstone to stay focused on your larger vision. | - Reignites passion and motivation - Helps overcome doubts - Reinforces long-term vision |
| Mindfulnes s Reset Timer | A reminder to practice mindfulness to stay grounded in the present moment. | Set a timer for daily mindfulness practice (5-10 minutes) to reset, breathe, and refocus during stressful moments. | To practice mindfulness and remain grounded in the present moment, reducing stress and promoting focus. | 1. Set a timer for 5-10 minutes. 2. Sit in a quiet space and focus on your breath. 3. If your mind wanders, gently bring it back to your breathing. | - Reduces stress and anxiety - Improves focus and clarity - Encourages emotional regulation |
| Self-Compassio n Letter | A letter written to yourself, offering understandin g, forgiveness, and encourageme nt during difficult times. | Write a letter to yourself after a setback, acknowledgin g the challenge, and offering words of comfort and compassion. | To offer yourself understandin g, forgiveness, and compassion during difficult times, fostering self-love. | 1. After a setback, write a letter to yourself expressing understanding and kindness. 2. Acknowledge your pain, but also encourage growth and healing. 3. Read the letter when you're feeling down. | - Encourages self-acceptance - Reduces self-criticism - Boosts emotional healing and resilience |

This table serves as a handy reference, providing actionable strategies to reinforce your resilience and embark on the path of self-redemption. The tools listed here can be easily incorporated into daily life, helping you transform adversity into opportunity and emerge from challenges stronger and more empowered.

**Summary: Embracing Resilience and Self-Redemption**

Building resilience and practicing self-redemption is a journey that requires intentional effort, self-reflection, and the willingness to embrace personal growth. The tools outlined in this chapter are designed to empower you to navigate life's challenges with strength, clarity, and purpose. By incorporating these tools into your daily routine, you can shift your perspective, overcome setb"

The tools shared in this chapter empower us to transform these struggles into growth, learning, and redemption opportunities. Through intentional actions, self-reflection, and a positive mindset, we shape our future outcomes, emerging stronger, wiser, and more resilient.

As you continue your journey, remember that resilience is not a trait but a practice. With **every challenge, you are shaping the person you are meant to be.**

Whether you are facing personal adversity, recovering from failure, or striving to achieve your goals, these tools provide the practical strategies needed to cultivate resilience

Resilience is the ultimate testament to human strength and perseverance. By applying the tools outlined in this chapter, you

unlock your inner potential, turning challenges into catalysts for growth and self-redemption. These tools empower you to rise above adversity, embrace failure as a stepping stone, and forge a path toward the life you envision. Each step you take is not just a move forward; it is an affirmation that no matter the storm, you have the strength to weather it and emerge stronger.

> *"Resilience is not about overcoming but becoming."* —
> **Sharon Salzberg**

By embracing resilience, you not only shape your outcome, but you inspire others to do the same. Your journey of self-redemption becomes a beacon of hope for those around you, showing them that there is always a way forward no matter the obstacle.

# Chapter 8:

# Resilience Unleashed

*"Courage doesn't always roar. Sometimes courage is the quiet voice at the end of the day saying, 'I will try again tomorrow.'"*
—Mary Anne Radmacher

**Planted Potential: The Seed Within**

Resilience often resembles a seed buried beneath the surface, hidden from view but full of potential. At first glance, it may seem small and insignificant, yet within its shell lies the blueprint for growth, strength, and transformation. Much like a seed, resilience doesn't emerge fully formed; instead, it requires the right conditions—nourishment, patience, and persistence—to break through the soil and thrive.

*Cracking Open*

In the beginning, seeds appear lifeless, much like the resilience we sometimes overlook within ourselves. They rest beneath layers of doubt, fear, and uncertainty, waiting for a spark—a moment of belief or action—to stir them awake. This process doesn't happen overnight. Seeds must first soften and crack open, allowing new life to push through their protective shells. Similarly, resilience requires us to let go of comfort and security, trusting that growth can come from what feels like breaking.

### *The Soil Around Us*

The soil represents our environment—the people, habits, and thoughts we surround ourselves with. Seeds need fertile ground to take root, and resilience also thrives in an atmosphere of support, positivity, and intention. Toxic environments, like dry and compacted soil, can stifle growth, while nurturing spaces encourage it to flourish. This is why resilience often begins with assessing where we're planted and making changes if the soil no longer serves us.

### *Drop by Drop*

Once planted, seeds need water to grow, much like resilience requires nourishment in the form of self-care, encouragement, and practice. A seed doesn't receive a single drop of water and immediately sprout into a towering tree. It must be watered consistently, drop by drop, trusting that each moment of care is bringing it closer to its potential. In the same way, resilience grows through small, consistent actions—choosing to get back up after a setback, practicing self-discipline, and taking steps toward progress even when results aren't immediately visible.

### Reaching for Light: Guided by Purpose

Light also plays a vital role. Seeds bend and stretch toward the sun, trusting it as a source of energy and direction. Similarly, resilience leans toward hope, purpose, and vision. It is drawn to goals, dreams, and values, using them as guiding lights during difficult times. Without direction, resilience can wither, much like a seed left in darkness. Setting goals provides clarity, acting as the light that pulls us forward, even when the path feels uncertain.

Yet, growth often begins in darkness. Seeds must first push through the soil, navigating resistance as they strive for the surface. This stage mirrors the challenges we face when building resilience. Growth isn't easy, and the process can feel uncomfortable, especially when we're digging through setbacks, fears, or failures. However, much like roots anchor a plant while it rises, resilience develops in these hidden moments of struggle. It's the unseen work—choosing to believe in ourselves, pushing through resistance, and showing up even when it's hard—that sets the foundation for lasting strength.

**Fragile Beginnings: The First Signs of Growth**

As the seed emerges, its first leaves unfold, fragile yet determined. This is where resilience takes shape. Early growth often feels delicate, and doubts can creep in, much like storms threaten young plants. Yet, it's during this stage that resilience gains strength through persistence. Facing obstacles, weathering criticism, and pushing forward despite setbacks toughens us, much like wind and rain fortify a plant's stem.

Over time, what began as a fragile sprout grows taller, stronger, and more rooted. Resilience, too, deepens as we continue to nourish it. Each challenge faced and overcome strengthens its foundation, allowing it to weather even greater storms. However, growth isn't always linear. Just as plants experience periods of dormancy, resilience may feel stagnant at times. These pauses aren't signs of failure but moments of preparation—an opportunity to gather strength before the next stage of growth.

Consider the tree that endures harsh winters, its leaves falling away as it conserves energy. Though it may appear lifeless, beneath the

surface, its roots are growing deeper, preparing for the spring. Resilience operates the same way. Times of struggle, rest, or reflection often precede moments of breakthrough. Instead of fearing stillness, we can learn to trust it, recognizing it as part of the process.

**Bending Without Breaking: Flexibility**

Resilience, like a plant, also adapts. It bends with the wind instead of breaking, adjusts its growth patterns to find sunlight, and draws nutrients from different sources when needed. This adaptability is key to resilience, allowing us to remain flexible without losing strength. Rather than resisting change, we can learn to grow with it, finding new ways to thrive in unexpected circumstances.

*Progress in Different Seasons*

It's also important to remember that not all seeds grow at the same pace. Some sprout quickly, while others take weeks or even months to push through the soil. Resilience, too, unfolds in its own time. Comparing our growth to others can leave us feeling discouraged, but every journey is unique. The oak tree may take years to reach its full height, but its strength and endurance make the wait worthwhile.

**Pruning for Growth: Letting Go to Move Forward**

Growth also requires pruning. Gardeners trim plants to remove dead branches and redirect energy toward healthier growth. In the same way, building resilience often involves letting go of what no longer serves us— unhealthy habits, limiting beliefs, or toxic relationships. Pruning can feel painful, but it creates space for new opportunities and stronger growth.

## Bearing Fruit: Turning Effort Into Results

As resilience continues to grow, it eventually bears fruit—achievements, wisdom, and personal breakthroughs. Yet, the process doesn't end there. Just as plants produce seeds to continue their life cycle, resilience inspires us to help others grow. Sharing our stories, offering encouragement, and supporting those who are struggling can create ripples of growth, planting seeds of resilience in those around us.

At its core, resilience is not just about surviving—it's about thriving. It's about recognizing that growth happens in seasons, that progress requires patience, and that setbacks often hold the greatest lessons. Like seeds, we are designed to grow, but it's up to us to create the right conditions for that growth.

## Awakening Potential: The Start of Something Greater

So, what does it take to awaken resilience?

It takes patience to trust the process, even when growth isn't visible. It takes courage to break through the surface, knowing that challenges will come. It takes consistency, watering our potential with small, intentional actions. And it takes vision—keeping our eyes on the light even when the path feels uncertain.

Resilience isn't built in moments of ease but in moments of effort. It grows each time we choose action over hesitation, progress over comfort, and belief over doubt. Much like a tree that stands tall despite the storm, resilience reminds us that strength isn't about avoiding challenges but about growing through them.

And just like seeds, we carry everything we need to grow within us. The potential is already there, waiting to be awakened. All it takes is the decision to start—the first drop of water, the first stretch toward the light—and the commitment to keep going

## Bravery in Dormancy: Awakening Inner Strength

Now, about bravery, it is often mistaken for an absence of fear, but true bravery thrives amidst uncertainty and doubt. It lies in the willingness to face discomfort, challenge limitations, and take steps forward even when the outcome is uncertain.

For many, bravery is a dormant force, quietly waiting for an opportunity to surface. Yet, it is always present, ready to be called upon when we decide to move beyond fear.

Dormant bravery isn't weakness—it's potential. Think of it as a fire waiting to be kindled. When life feels overwhelming, it is this latent bravery that propels us to try, to persist, and to grow. For example, consider Mia, a single mother who long dreamed of starting her own bakery. Fear of failure and self-doubt kept her dreams dormant for years. It wasn't until she started taking small, brave steps—attending a baking workshop, experimenting with recipes, and finally selling cupcakes at a local market—that her dormant bravery transformed into confidence. Today, Mia's bakery is a thriving community space, and she credits her success to those initial steps of courage.

**Reflection Prompt:**

- What area of your life feels dormant?

  Write down one small, brave action you can take this week to awaken it.

_____

_____

_____

_____

**Building Confidence through Action—Examples**

Confidence isn't something we're born with; it's a skill cultivated through repeated actions and incremental successes. Each time we step outside our comfort zone, we strengthen our belief in our abilities. Confidence grows not from the absence of failure but from the determination to keep going despite it.

Take Alex, for instance, a recent graduate who felt unprepared for the workforce. With every job rejection, his confidence dwindled, until he decided to focus on what he could control: his skills. Alex committed to learning something new every day, from online courses to mock interviews. Slowly but surely, his efforts paid off. When he finally landed his first job, it wasn't just his resume that had improved—it was his confidence in his ability to adapt and persevere.

Sophia always dreamed of running her own event-planning business, but the fear of failure held her back. After being laid off from her corporate job, she found herself at a crossroads—sink into self-doubt or take a leap of faith. She started small, organizing birthday parties for friends and volunteering at community events to build her portfolio. With each successful event, her confidence grew. She also took online marketing courses to sharpen her skills and reached out to local businesses for partnerships. Within a year, Sophia had transformed her side hustle into a thriving business. Her resilience wasn't just about surviving job loss—it was about creating opportunities where none existed before.

Daniel, a former athlete, suffered a severe knee injury that derailed his career and left him battling depression. For months, he struggled with feelings of helplessness and loss of identity. One day, he made a decision to focus on what he could rebuild instead of mourning what he had lost. He started physical therapy, committed to a daily stretching routine, and slowly regained strength. At the same time, he shifted his focus to nutrition and fitness training, eventually becoming a certified personal trainer. Today, Daniel helps others recover from injuries, turning his own setbacks into a source of strength and inspiration.

Maya had always excelled in school until she failed her final exams during her freshman year of college. The failure shook her confidence, and she began doubting her abilities. Determined to rise above her setback, Maya sought tutoring, joined study groups, and developed better time-management strategies. She also focused on improving her mindset, repeating affirmations and visualizing success before exams.

By the end of the following semester, she had not only passed her retakes but earned top marks. Her resilience transformed failure into fuel, proving that setbacks can be setups for comebacks.

These stories illustrate how resilience grows through deliberate action, persistence, and adaptability. Alex, Sophia, Daniel, and Maya faced setbacks that could have defined them, yet they chose to rise above their challenges. Alex rebuilt his confidence by improving his skills, Sophia turned job loss into an entrepreneurial success, Daniel transformed injury into purpose, and Maya reclaimed her academic path after failure. Their journeys highlight that resilience isn't about avoiding obstacles but confronting them with courage and determination. Each setback became a stepping stone, proving that growth often begins in moments of struggle and flourishes through persistence and intentional effort.

**Activity:** Confidence Ladder

1. Write down a goal you want to achieve.

 

2. Break it into smaller, manageable steps.

 

3. Celebrate each step as you complete it.

 

o Example: If your goal is to deliver a public speech, start by practicing in front of a mirror, then with close friends, and finally in a small group setting.

**Key Insight:**

Confidence isn't the result of **never failing**—it's the result of **continuing to try**.

**The Power of Self-Discipline**

Dreams often start as sparks of inspiration, but without discipline, they tend to fade into wishful thinking. Self-discipline is what fuels the journey from imagination to reality. It's not about being perfect every step of the way—it's about showing up, even when progress feels slow or motivation runs low. While enthusiasm might light the path at first, it's the steady rhythm of discipline that keeps us moving forward when excitement wears off.

More than just a habit, self-discipline shapes how we approach challenges. It reminds us to focus on what truly matters, especially when distractions or doubts try to steal our attention. Instead of waiting for the "perfect moment," discipline teaches us to start where we are and take one small step at a time. Those steps, however ordinary they may seem, build momentum that eventually carries us across the finish line.

But discipline isn't just about actions—it's also about trust. Every time we follow through on a promise we've made to ourselves, we strengthen our belief in our ability to keep going. That trust becomes a source of confidence, helping us face obstacles without backing down. It's not about grinding ourselves into exhaustion; it's about staying committed, even on the days when results aren't immediate.

At the same time, discipline requires patience. Growth doesn't always come with quick rewards, and the process can feel frustrating. Yet, sticking with it teaches us to focus on progress rather than perfection. It shows us that small efforts, repeated over time, lead to bigger results than sudden bursts of inspiration ever could.

You can say that discipline opens doors. It gives us the freedom to pursue what we want, knowing we have the tools to get there. It shifts our focus from what we can't control to what we can, turning effort into achievement and ideas into reality. Instead of waiting for things to change, discipline retells us that we have the power to create that change—one step at a time.

**Tool:** The Discipline Tracker

1. Identify a goal and choose one small habit that supports it.

_____

2. Create a tracker (physical or digital) to record your progress.

_____

3. Reward yourself for consistency, not perfection.

_____

**Mantra:**

"Small, consistent actions lead to extraordinary results."

**Activities to Boost Self-Esteem**

1. **The Mirror Exercise**

    o  Purpose: Cultivate self-acceptance.

    o  Instructions: Stand in front of a mirror and say three positive affirmations about yourself daily.

    o  Example: "I am capable. I am growing. I am enough."

2. **Gratitude for Strengths**

    o  Purpose: Shift focus to what you do well.

    o  Instructions: Write down three things you did well each day, no matter how small.

3. **The "Fear Inventory"**

    o  Purpose: Address self-doubt head-on.

    o  Instructions: List your fears and next to each, write one action you can take to confront it.

    o  Example: Fear: Public speaking. Action: Join a local Toastmasters group.

4. **Achievement Jar**

    o  Purpose: Celebrate progress.

o  Instructions: Write each achievement on a small note and place it in a jar. Review these notes whenever you need a confidence boost.

## Realizing Dreams Through Resilience

Dreams require a blend of bravery, confidence, and discipline. These qualities don't appear overnight—they are cultivated through small, intentional steps. Resilience acts as the foundation, enabling us to persevere through setbacks and adapt to challenges.

Think of Emma, who aspired to run a marathon. She wasn't a runner, but she committed to starting with short walks, then jogs, and eventually training runs. Each step required resilience—on days when her legs ached, when the weather was unkind, or when doubt crept in. But her discipline kept her going, and crossing the finish line wasn't just the realization of a dream—it was a testament to her resilience.

## Key Takeaway:

Resilience isn't a destination; it's the process of showing up for yourself daily.

## Final Reflections

As you unleash your resilience, remember: bravery begins in small, quiet steps; confidence grows through repeated action; and discipline is the steady hand that guides you toward your dreams. Each challenge you face is an opportunity to strengthen these qualities.

**Reflection Questions:**

1. What dream have you set aside, and what small step can you take today to move toward it?

_____

_____

_____

_____

2. How can you incorporate self-discipline into your daily routine?

_____

_____

_____

_____

3. What activity from this chapter will you try this week to boost your confidence?

_____

_____

_____

_____

Your resilience is already within you, waiting to be allowed to run free. By infusing bravery into dormancy, building confidence step by step, and practicing self-discipline, you can transform dreams into reality and challenges into growth opportunities. The table below serves as a practical guide to help you take intentional steps toward building confidence through action. It highlights key stages, outlines the purpose of each, and emphasizes the outcomes that contribute to personal growth.

## Table: Building Confidence

| Step | Action | Purpose | Outcome |
| --- | --- | --- | --- |
| **1. Identify a Goal** | Write down a specific goal you want to achieve. | Provides clarity and direction, making the goal more tangible. | Builds focus and sets a starting point for progress. |
| **2. Break It Down** | Divide the goal into smaller, manageable tasks. | Reduces overwhelm and makes the process feel more achievable. | Creates actionable steps that lead to steady progress. |
| **3. Take the First Step** | Begin with the easiest task to build momentum. | Encourages action and minimizes procrastination. | Builds confidence through small wins. |
| **4. Track Progress** | Use a journal or tracker to monitor accomplishments daily. | Reinforces commitment and highlights growth over time. | Provides motivation by showcasing progress. |
| **5. Celebrate Milestones** | Reward yourself for completing each step, no matter how small. | Reinforces positive behavior and creates a sense of achievement. | Boosts morale and keeps motivation high. |
| **6. Learn from Setbacks** | Reflect on challenges and identify lessons from failures. | Shifts perspective from failure to learning opportunities. | Strengthens adaptability and mental resilience. |
| **7. Adjust and Continue** | Reassess strategies and make adjustments as needed. | Ensures flexibility and keeps focus aligned with evolving goals. | Maintains momentum even when obstacles arise. |

*"Resilience isn't about waiting for the perfect moment; it's about creating it through courage, consistency, and confidence."*

# Chapter 9:

# A Remaining Strength

*"Strength does not come from winning. Your struggles develop your strengths. When you go through hardships and decide not to surrender, that is strength."*—Arnold Schwarzenegger

Life is never still. It flows like a river, sometimes calm and steady, other times wild and unpredictable, carving new paths as it moves forward. Much like the tides, it rises and falls, carrying us through moments of growth, loss, and renewal.

Change is inevitable, often arriving without warning, yet within each of us lies an enduring strength—a quiet force that deepens with every experience and allows us to adapt, endure, and transform.

Think of a tree standing tall through every season. In spring, it bursts with new life, stretching its branches toward the sun. During summer, it stands firm, basking in its growth. By autumn, it lets go of what it no longer needs, shedding its leaves as a preparation for rest. In winter, stripped bare, it appears lifeless, but beneath the surface, its roots dig deeper, gathering strength for the next bloom. Its survival isn't found in resisting the seasons but in trusting each phase as necessary for its growth. Similarly, our ability to thrive depends on how we respond to life's ever-changing cycles.

Maya Angelou once said,

*I can be changed by what happens to me. But I refuse to be reduced by it."*

These words remind us that challenges may form us, but they don't have to define us. It is through adaptation, reflection, and steady effort that we learn to rise stronger, turning unexpected shifts into opportunities for personal growth. Similarly, strength of character isn't something we're born with—it's developed over time, much like muscles that grow stronger with use. It requires care and attention, built through self-reflection, consistent effort, and trust in the process. Challenges are not disruptions to our path but opportunities to grow, adapt, and uncover the potential that has been inside us all along. Life's movements, whether sudden or gradual, don't signal endings but new beginnings waiting to develop.

Take Emma, for example. After losing her job, she could have allowed disappointment to define her. Instead, she saw it as a chance to reinvent herself. She enrolled in courses, developed new skills, and eventually built a business of her own. Her success didn't come from avoiding setbacks but from learning through them and stepping forward even when the outcome was unclear.

**Reflection Prompt:**

- Think about a time when you faced a significant challenge. How did you adapt and grow as a result? What lessons did that experience teach you about your ability to endure?

**Rising to Changing Times**

The world is always changing. Technology advances at an incredible pace, reshaping the way we live, work, and connect.

*Innovations*

Innovations that once seemed like science fiction have become part of everyday life, influencing careers, industries, and relationships. While this rapid evolution can feel exciting, it can also be unsettling. To keep up, we need more than awareness—we need adaptability. Just as technology updates to stay useful, we too must grow and evolve to meet the demands of an ever-changing world.

As artificial intelligence, automation, and digital tools continue to advance, they bring opportunities we never could have imagined. At the same time, these developments have disrupted long-standing practices, leaving some industries struggling to adjust. Jobs that once felt secure have vanished, replaced by machines and systems that operate faster and more efficiently. Understandably, these changes can feel overwhelming. However, when viewed with the right perspective, they reveal opportunities rather than barriers. Remaining flexible and open to learning doesn't just help us survive—it positions us to thrive in a world that never stops moving forward.

Take Mark, for instance. After spending years working in a factory, he suddenly found himself unemployed when automation took over his role. The routine he had depended on was gone, and uncertainty filled its place. At first, the change felt like failure—a door closing on

everything familiar. Yet Mark refused to let it define him. Instead, he took action, enrolling in night classes, learning to code, and gradually building new skills.

Of course, the process wasn't easy. Mark faced moments of doubt, questioning whether he could succeed in an entirely new field. Nevertheless, he stuck with it, focusing on one step at a time. What started as a way to survive eventually became something more—a passion for building programs and solving problems. Today, Mark works as a software developer, using the very technology that once threatened his job to create new solutions. Looking back, he doesn't see his layoff as the end of the road. Instead, he views it as the push he needed to grow into something better.

Mark's experience highlights an important truth—change doesn't have to mean failure.

While technological progress may disrupt the way things are, it also opens doors to new opportunities. The key is how we respond. Do we resist change, or do we choose to work with it? In today's fast-paced world, adaptability isn't just a helpful trait—it's essential. Whether we're learning new software, exploring artificial intelligence, or picking up unfamiliar tools, we are constantly challenged to step outside our comfort zones.

Think of it like upgrading a phone or computer. Every so often, devices need updates to keep up with changing demands and stay functional. We're no different. By staying curious and willing to learn, we can

ensure that we're prepared for whatever comes next. Rather than fearing change, we can approach it as an opportunity—one that allows us to grow, improve, and uncover strengths we didn't know we had.

As technology continues to shape the future, our ability to adapt will determine not only how we fit into this shifting world but also how we define success.

Growth rarely happens in comfort. Instead, it comes from stepping into uncertainty, pushing ourselves to learn, and viewing change not as a setback but as a chance to build something even better.

> *"It is not the strongest of the species that survive, nor the most intelligent, but the one most responsive to change."* — Charles Darwin

*What does it take to adapt in today's fast-paced, AI-driven world?*

Consider Sarah, a customer service representative who feared that artificial intelligence would make her job obsolete. Her company began using AI chatbots to handle routine inquiries, leaving Sarah uncertain about her role. Instead of resisting the shift, she chose to grow with it. YES!

Sarah learned how to operate and monitor the chatbot system, ensuring it ran smoothly and could handle more complex requests. As her knowledge grew, Sarah took it a step further. She completed online courses in AI management and became the go-to person in her company for improving chatbot performance and training new employees on how to collaborate with AI tools. What initially felt like

a threat to her career became an opportunity for advancement. Today, Sarah is not only more skilled but also more confident in her ability to stay relevant as technology continues to evolve.

This instance highlights how adapting to change, rather than fearing it, opens doors we may not have seen before. You see, AI isn't just replacing tasks—it's creating entirely new roles and industries as well.

**The real question**—are we willing to step forward, learn, and discover where those new opportunities might lead?

**Activity: Building Adaptability**

1.  **List a Recent Change:** Write down a recent change in your life—positive or negative.

    _____

    _____

    _____

2.  **Identify Your Response:** Reflect on how you initially reacted to the change.

    _____

    _____

    Did you resist, embrace, or avoid it?

    _____

    _____

3. **Explore Possibilities:** Write down one way you can view the change as an opportunity rather than a setback.

_____

_____

_____

_____

**Key Insight:**

*Change is inevitable, but how we respond to it determines whether it can truly breaks us/build us.*

### 1. Cultivating a Growth Mindset

A growth mindset sees challenges not as threats but as opportunities to learn and improve. Instead of asking, "Why is this happening to me?" shift to, "What can this teach me?"

### Tool: The Growth Journal

• Write down one challenge you faced each week and reflect on the lessons it offered.

_____

_____

- Track how your mindset shifts over time as you reinterpret setbacks as growth opportunities.

_____

_____

## 2. Developing Mental Flexibility

Rigid thinking is like driving down a road with no exits. Even when traffic backs up or a detour is clearly needed, it keeps pushing straight ahead, hoping things will somehow clear up. Mental flexibility, on the other hand, is like having a GPS that quickly reroutes you when obstacles appear. It doesn't panic—it just recalculates and finds another way forward.

Life throws curveballs—job losses, breakups, or plans that suddenly fall apart. If we're stuck on one way of doing things, it's easy to feel cornered. But being mentally flexible means pulling out the map, figuring out what still works, and taking another route. It's not about having all the answers; it's about being willing to ask different questions and try something new.

Think about how trees bend in the wind. They don't snap because they're loose enough to sway but strong enough to stay rooted. That's the balance mental flexibility gives us—it's not about giving up, but knowing when to switch tactics without losing sight of what matters. Whether it's picking up a new skill, looking at a problem from another angle, or scrapping a plan that's no longer working, adapting doesn't

just help us get through tough spots. It helps us keep going without wasting time waiting for things to go back to how they were.

**Exercise:**

**The "What If?" Scenario**

1.  Write down a fear or worry you have about the future.

    _____

    _____

2.  List three possible outcomes—best-case, worst-case, and most likely scenario.

    _____

    _____

3.  Develop a plan for how you'll handle each outcome.

    _____

    _____

This exercise reduces anxiety and boosts confidence by preparing you to face uncertainty head-on.

**3. Building Emotional Endurance**

- **What Is Emotional Endurance?**
  - The ability to stay grounded and balanced during life's challenges.

- o A skill that helps you face emotional storms without losing control.

- **What It's Not:**

  - o Suppressing feelings or pretending everything is fine.

  - o Ignoring emotions or pushing them aside.

- **What It Does:**

  - o Encourages processing emotions in a healthy, constructive way.

  - o Allows you to feel without being overwhelmed.

  - o Helps you respond thoughtfully instead of reacting impulsively.

- **Why It Matters:**

  - o Builds mental strength to face setbacks, grief, or uncertainty.

  - o Promotes long-term growth by turning struggles into learning opportunities.

  - o Keeps you grounded, even when life feels chaotic.

- **How to Build It:**

  - o Practice self-reflection to understand your triggers and responses.

  - o Use mindfulness techniques like deep breathing and journaling.

- o Focus on solutions rather than dwelling on problems.

- o Lean on trusted relationships for support when emotions feel heavy.

- **Important Take-out:**
  Emotional endurance isn't about avoiding the storm—it's about learning how to stand firm and face it.

## Tool: Emotional Check-Ins

- Schedule regular "check-in" times to evaluate your emotions.

- Use mindfulness techniques, like deep breathing or meditation, to regulate intense emotions.

Rate how you're feeling on a scale of 1-10

## 4. Strengthening Connections— Buffer Against Stress

Softness is often rooted in relationships—especially supportive connections that jog our memory that we're not alone and provide a buffer against stress.

### *Ways to Strengthen Connections:*

- o **Reach Out Regularly:** Make time for calls, coffee chats, or simple check-ins.

- o **Be Vulnerable:** Share your struggles openly to deepen trust.

- o **Offer Support Too:** Relationships thrive on mutual care, so be there for others as well.

- ○ **Expand Your Circle:** Join clubs, networking groups, or online communities to meet new people.

Strong connections help you survive tough times—they recap you that you don't have to face them alone. Never...

Write down what's contributing to that feeling of strength...

_____

_____

_____

_____

_____

**Activity: Building Your Resilience Network**

- • List people you can reach out to during challenging times.

_____

_____

- • Set a goal to check in with one person this week—whether through a coffee date, phone call, or message.

_____

_____

## The Power in Practice

Personal growth often starts with self-reflection. Taking time to look back on experiences helps us notice patterns, track progress, and pinpoint areas where we can improve. It's not about being overly critical—it's about recognizing what works, what doesn't, and where we can make adjustments. Regular reflection creates space for growth, making it easier to focus on progress rather than perfection.

### *Sarah's Story:*

After going through a painful divorce, Sarah felt lost and uncertain about what her future held. Her confidence was shaken, and simple tasks often felt overwhelming. Determined to regain her footing, she picked up a notebook and began journaling every day.

At first, her entries were raw and unfiltered, filled with frustration and sadness. But as time went on, Sarah began to notice patterns—days when she felt a little stronger and days when she struggled. Instead of being hard on herself, she started celebrating the small wins, like going for a walk, cooking a healthy meal, or reaching out to a friend.

Little by little, her journal shifted from a place of pain to a source of strength. It became a tool to track her progress, highlight what lifted her spirits, and remind her of how far she'd come. Through this process, Sarah not only healed but also rebuilt her sense of purpose and confidence.

You see, Sarah's journey shows that reflection isn't about dwelling on the past—it's about powerful tools for growth. They help us acknowledge struggles without judgment, celebrate small victories, and create a clearer path forward.

**Reflection Prompt:**

- What small victories can you celebrate today? Write down three accomplishments, no matter how minor they seem.

_____

_____

_____

_____

_____

## No Finish Line

Unlike achievements that come with a certificate or a trophy, resilience doesn't end with a ceremony. It's a lifelong process, constantly tested and renewed through life's changes. What matters most is the willingness to keep showing up, even when the path is unclear.

### *Mantra:*

"I am a work in progress, and every step forward strengthens me."

It is not about reaching perfection—it's about remaining open to growth, even in moments of doubt. Whether you're facing a personal loss, a career change, or a new chapter in life, your resilience will carry you forward, adapting as you do.

*Your strength is not measured by the absence of hardship but by your ability to keep moving forward.*

**Final Echoes: Owning Your Strength**

As you reflect on your journey, remember this: Flexibility isn't about avoiding struggles—it's about learning from them to continue to rise.

**Consideration:**

1. What has been the most significant challenge in your life so far? How did you overcome it?

_____

_____

_____

_____

_____

2. What steps can you take to build resilience for future challenges?

_____

_____

_____

_____

_____

3. Who or what inspires you to keep going, even when times get tough?

_____

_____

_____

_____

_____

_____

_____

**Takeaways:**

Resilience doesn't have an expiration date. It's a remaining strength that grows with every challenge you face and every victory you celebrate.

*"Strength doesn't come from never falling; it comes from getting back up—again and again, for as long as it takes."*

# Chapter 10:

# Nurturing Emotional

# Intelligence

*"It is very important to understand that emotional intelligence is not the opposite of intelligence, it is not the triumph of heart over head—it is the unique intersection of both."* — David Caruso

## Power of Emotional Intelligence

Emotions are at the core of what makes us human. They color how we experience the world, influence how we make decisions, and shape our relationships. Yet, many of us grow up without learning how to truly understand or manage them. We're often told to "keep it together" or "stop overreacting," leaving us ill-equipped to face emotional challenges. Emotional intelligence changes that.

It isn't about suppressing feelings—it's about recognizing, understanding, and using them in ways that support growth and connection. It's the ability to stay calm under pressure, handle conflicts with grace, and motivate ourselves and others when times get tough. In essence, emotional intelligence is less about reacting to the world and more about responding to it thoughtfully.

You see, emotional intelligence acts as a secret weapon against life's trials.

## What Is Emotional Intelligence?

Think of emotional intelligence as a personal compass. It guides you through the ups and downs of life by helping you identify what you're feeling, why you're feeling it, and how to respond.

Emotional intelligence is made up of four key components:

1. **Self-Awareness** – Recognizing and understanding your emotions as they arise.

2. **Self-Management** – Controlling impulses, adapting to change, and staying calm under stress.

3. **Social Awareness** – Recognizing the emotions of others and showing empathy.

4. **Relationship Management** – Using emotional insight to build stronger connections and resolve conflicts effectively.

These skills don't come naturally for most people—they are learned through practice. Like building muscle, strengthening emotional intelligence requires effort and consistency.

The good news?

Once developed, these skills become invaluable tools for managing challenges and turning obstacles into opportunities.

### The Science Behind

Psychologist **Daniel Goleman**, who popularized the concept, highlights five key components that form the foundation of EI:

- **Self-Awareness** – Recognizing your own emotions and their impact.

- **Self-Regulation** – Managing emotional reactions in constructive ways.

- **Motivation** – Using emotions to stay driven toward goals.

- **Empathy** – Understanding and connecting with others' emotions.

- **Social Skills** – Building and maintaining meaningful relationships.

Research from the **American Psychological Association (APA)** shows that people with higher emotional intelligence experience:

- **Lower stress levels** due to improved coping strategies.

- **Faster recovery from setbacks** because of emotional resilience.

- **Better decision-making** by balancing emotion with logic.

- **Stronger relationships** through empathy and effective communication.

Neurologically, EI works by regulating signals from the **amygdala**, which processes fear and stress, through the **prefrontal cortex**, which governs reasoning and control. This balance prevents impulsive reactions and promotes thoughtful responses.

### *Signals, Not Setbacks*

Psychological research suggests that emotions aren't problems to fix—they're signals to interpret. For example:

- **Anxiety** can highlight areas where more preparation is needed.

- **Anger** might signal crossed boundaries or unmet expectations.

- **Sadness** can point to unresolved loss or areas that need healing.

By treating emotions as **data** rather than obstacles, we can respond with purpose instead of avoidance.

A study published in the *Journal of Applied Psychology* found that employees who practiced **emotional regulation techniques** reported:

- **Greater job satisfaction.**

- **Higher productivity levels.**

- **Improved teamwork and collaboration.**

This supports the idea that managing emotions doesn't require suppression but **channeling them constructively** to fuel action.

**Dr. Susan David**, author of *Emotional Agility*, emphasizes the need to:

1. **Label Emotions:** Naming feelings reduces their intensity and brings clarity.

2. **Accept Emotions:** Allow yourself to feel without judgment to process them properly.

3. **Align with Values:** Focus emotional responses on actions that reflect your long-term values and goals.

For instance, anxiety before a presentation can be reframed as **excitement**, motivating preparation instead of avoidance. Similarly, anger can be turned into assertiveness rather than reactivity.

## The Story of Ben: From Reaction to Reflection

Ben had always struggled to control his emotions. When things didn't go his way at work, he'd lash out in frustration, damaging relationships with colleagues. At home, he often shut down during arguments, avoiding conversations that felt too overwhelming. Over time, these habits left him isolated and stuck.

One day, after a particularly heated exchange with his boss, Ben decided he needed a change. He began reading about emotional intelligence and realized that his reactions weren't the problem—it was his lack of emotional awareness. Determined to improve, Ben started practicing mindfulness, pausing to reflect before reacting, and journaling about his feelings.

As the weeks passed, Ben noticed subtle changes. He became more aware of his triggers and learned to step away when emotions felt too strong. Instead of shouting during disagreements, he started asking questions to understand the other person's perspective. Over time, his relationships improved, and so did his confidence. Ben's transformation didn't happen overnight, but it showed him the power of emotional intelligence. By learning to manage his emotions, he didn't just change how he interacted with others—he changed how he saw himself.

## Structure Emotional Awareness: Exercises and Practices

Here are some exercises to sharpen emotional awareness and boost emotional intelligence:

### 1. The Emotional Journal

- **Purpose:** Track emotions and uncover patterns.

- **Instructions:**

1. Spend 5 minutes each day writing down how you felt during the day.

_____

_____

2. Identify triggers that caused specific emotions—was it a situation, a person, or a thought?

_____

_____

3. Write how you reacted and whether it was helpful or harmful.

_____

_____

- **Outcome:** Improves emotional recognition and helps you identify areas for growth.

## 2. The 3-Second Pause

- **Purpose:** Develop emotional control before responding.

- **Instructions:**

1. When faced with a stressful situation, pause and take three deep breaths.

2. Ask yourself, "What am I feeling right now?"

_____

_____

3. Respond only after identifying your emotions.

- **Outcome:** Reduces impulsive reactions and promotes thoughtful responses.

## 3. Name It to Tame It

- **Purpose:** Label emotions to understand them better.

- **Instructions:**

1. When you feel strong emotions, give them a name—anger, sadness, joy, anxiety.

2. Acknowledge the feeling without judgment.

3. Explore why you feel that way and what it's telling you.

- **Outcome:** Increases emotional clarity and reduces the intensity of negative emotions.

**Your Space:**

_____

_____

_____

_____

_____

_____

## Recognizing Emotions in Others

### Key Steps to Develop Empathy:

- **Observe Body Language:** Pay attention to facial expressions, tone of voice, and gestures.

- **Listen Without Interrupting:** Focus on what the other person is saying rather than planning your response.

- **Ask Questions:** Show curiosity about their feelings and experiences.

- **Validate Emotions:** Let them know their feelings are seen and understood, even if you don't agree.

When we become more aware of what others feel, we improve our ability to build trust, resolve conflicts, and deepen connections. Thus, Emotional intelligence isn't just about understanding ourselves—it's also about tuning into the emotions of those around us.

## Case Study: Lisa's Empathy

### The Problem

- **Lisa's Strengths:** Highly analytical and results-driven.

- **The Challenge:**

  ○ Colleagues found her directness intimidating.

  ○ Friends felt unheard during personal conversations.

  ○ Struggled to connect emotionally with others.

### The Turning Point

Lisa decided to make a change by focusing on **active listening** and **empathy-building techniques**:

| Old Approach | New Approach |
|---|---|
| Jumped in with solutions before listening. | Listened fully before responding. |
| Focused only on logic and facts. | Acknowledged emotions before offering solutions. |
| Avoided emotional conversations. | Validated feelings using phrases like: |
|  | - *"That sounds frustrating."* |
|  | - *"I can see why you'd feel that way."* |

### The Results

| Personal Growth | Professional Growth |
|---|---|
| Built deeper connections with friends. | Gained trust and respect as a leader at work. |
| Became more empathetic and approachable. | Improved teamwork and collaboration in the workplace. |

| Personal Growth | Professional Growth |
|---|---|
| Created a safe space for others to open up. | Learned to resolve conflicts with better understanding. |

*Emotional intelligence doesn't erase emotions but channels them into growth opportunities.*

## Examples:

| Emotion | Reaction Before | Constructive Response Now |
|---|---|---|
| **Anxiety** | Avoided preparation. | Used anxiety as motivation to prepare thoroughly. |
| **Frustration** | Snapped at coworkers. | Took a break, then calmly discussed solutions. |
| **Disappointment** | Dwelled on failure. | Reflected on lessons and adjusted future plans. |

## *Carryout*

Lisa's story highlights that **emotional intelligence is a skill, not a trait.** By practicing empathy and reflection, we can transform our emotions into tools for **personal and professional growth**.

## Prompt:

What's one emotional response you can handle differently today? Write it down and plan a constructive response!

## Activity: Emotional Check-In Chart

| Emotion | Trigger | Reaction | Alternative Response |
|---------|---------|----------|---------------------|
| Anger | Missed deadline at work | Yelled at a coworker | Take a walk, then discuss solutions. |
| Anxiety | Upcoming presentation | Avoided practicing | Rehearse with a friend for feedback. |
| Sadness | Argument with a friend | Ignored calls and isolated myself | Write a letter to express your feelings. |

**Goal:** *Use this chart to reflect on emotional patterns and identify healthier responses.*

_____

_____

_____

_____

_____

_____

## The Link—Emotional Intelligence and Future Vision

What sets emotionally intelligent individuals apart isn't just how they handle present emotions—it's how they use those emotions to **project into the future**. Emotional intelligence helps us imagine possibilities, anticipate emotional obstacles, and prepare for them before they occur.

This forward-thinking approach creates a **vision-based resilience**—a mindset that doesn't wait for challenges to appear but actively prepares for them by visualizing positive outcomes and crafting strategies in advance.

- *Entrepreneurs* every so often face uncertainty—and failure.
  - o Emotionally intelligent entrepreneurs, however, tend to visualize their success and prepare mentally for setbacks, enabling them to stay calm and adaptable during crises.

### *Data, Not Drama*

One of the most unique aspects of emotional intelligence is its ability to **turn emotions into information rather than obstacles**. Instead of dismissing emotions as irrational or overwhelming, emotionally intelligent people treat them like **data points**—signals that provide insights into underlying needs, values, or boundaries.

For instance:

- **Jealousy** might reveal a hidden desire for recognition or growth.

- **Frustration** might indicate unmet expectations or unclear boundaries.

- **Guilt** may point to an internal conflict between values and actions.

By analyzing emotions in this way, we shift from being **reactive to reflective**, allowing emotions to guide decisions without derailing them.

## The Emotional Immune System

Emotional intelligence also acts as an **emotional immune system**—shielding us from the negative effects of stress while helping us bounce back from setbacks. Just as the body fights off infections and adapts to build immunity, EI helps us:

- Process emotional pain instead of avoiding it.

- Strengthen coping mechanisms through emotional awareness.

- Develop a **psychological buffer** against criticism, rejection, or failure.

This *emotional immunity* doesn't mean avoiding hardships but facing them with tools that make recovery faster and growth more intentional.

## Thoughts in Action

It isn't about being perfect—it's about becoming more intentional with how we respond to life's challenges. It's the ability to face emotions head-on, whether they're comfortable or uncomfortable, and use them to make decisions that align with who we want to be. It isn't about being unshaken by life—it's about learning how to stand tall while the storm passes. With each new step, you'll discover that emotions, when understood and managed, are not obstacles but powerful allies in your journey forward.

**Key Takeaway:** Emotional intelligence is not just a skill—it's a foundation for growth. It allows us to turn emotions into tools, setbacks into lessons, and challenges into opportunities for transformation.

**Reflection Questions:**

1. What emotion do you struggle with most, and how do you currently handle it?

   _____

2. How can you use emotional intelligence to improve your relationships?

   _____

3. What's one small step you can take today to sharpen your emotional awareness?

   _____

*"Mastering emotions isn't about silencing them—it's about learning to let them speak without letting them shout."*

# Chapter 11:

# The Influence of Relationships

*"Alone, we can do so little; together, we can do so much."* —
Helen Keller

Humans are inherently social beings. From the moment we are born, we seek connection—whether through family, friends, or communities. These relationships act as a lifeline during hardships and a foundation for growth and support.

While personal resilience helps us stand tall, it's often the relationships we build that keep us from falling when challenges feel overwhelming.

This chapter explores how relationships influence emotional, mental, and physical well-being. It highlights the role of supportive communities and safe spaces, not just as buffers against life's difficulties but as tools for transformation.

Through practical advice and strategies, we'll also examine how to create and sustain support networks, making connections a source of strength for ourselves and others.

Imagine this—you're climbing a rock wall, determined to reach the top. Your muscles are burning, sweat is pouring down your face, and for a moment, you think about letting go. But then, you hear your friends below, cheering you on, reminding you why you started.

That's what connection feels like. It doesn't erase the climb, but it makes it easier to keep going.

And let's face it, life can be messy. Jobs are lost, hearts are broken, and plans don't always pan out the way we hoped. In those moments, it's tempting to retreat, to shut everyone out and pretend we can handle it alone.

But isolation only makes the climb harder.

It's like trying to light a fire with wet wood—possible, but exhausting. On the other hand, reaching out to someone can feel like adding dry kindling. It sparks something—hope, relief, or even just the comfort of knowing someone's in it with you.

Sometimes, support looks like a friend who picks up the phone at midnight when you can't sleep. Other times, it's a neighbor who drops off groceries when you're too sick to leave the house. It might even be a stranger in a support group who listens and says, "Me too."

*Truth:* Resilience isn't built in isolation. It's built in circles—in conversations over coffee, in late-night calls, and in shared laughter and tears. Alone, we can stand for a while, but collected, we can stand for a generation.

### Researching Relations

Research has consistently shown that strong relationships improve mental and physical health.

Studies from the **American Psychological Association** reveal that individuals with supportive networks experience:

- **Lower stress levels** due to emotional validation.

- **Faster recovery from hardships** through shared problem-solving.

- **Improved mental health** by reducing feelings of loneliness and isolation.

- **Better resilience** against life's uncertainties through encouragement and accountability.

More than emotional comfort, relationships provide resources, such as shared knowledge, financial support, and even practical solutions like housing stability in times of need.

The ability to turn to someone for advice, shelter, or even a listening ear can make all the difference when facing personal or professional struggles.

### *The Story of Emily:*

Emily was a single mother of two who found herself facing one of the hardest times in her life. After losing her job, she had no savings to fall back on and eviction was right around the corner. The thought of not having a safe place for her kids kept her awake at night. She felt scared, overwhelmed, and unsure of what to do next.

At first, Emily thought about handling everything on her own, but deep down, she knew she needed help. Instead of shutting herself off,

she decided to reach out to a local support group for single parents. It wasn't easy to ask for help, but once she did, things began to change.

The group welcomed her with open arms. They offered emotional support and listened without judgment. More than that, they provided real solutions. They connected Emily with a temporary housing program so she and her kids wouldn't end up without a roof over their heads. They also helped her find job placement services to get back on her feet.

Emily started attending weekly meetings, and little by little, she felt a weight lift off her shoulders. She learned how to manage her budget, how to prepare for job interviews, and how to rebuild her confidence. Each meeting reminded her that she wasn't alone—that there were others who understood her struggles and wanted to see her succeed.

It wasn't an instant fix. Emily had to work hard, but the encouragement she received made it easier to keep going. Eventually, she found a job and moved into stable housing. Her situation improved, but what mattered most was the friendships she built along the way. The group didn't just help her through the tough times; they continued to cheer her on even after her crisis ended.

Emily's story shows just how powerful relationships can be. When everything seemed to be falling apart, it was the people she turned to who helped her rebuild.

A community is more than a group of people—it's a **shared space of trust, understanding, and common goals**.

Whether it's a neighborhood group, a faith-based circle, or an online forum, communities create:

- **Safe Spaces:** Where individuals feel heard and valued.

- **Problem-Solving Networks:** Offering collective wisdom and resources.

- **Accountability Systems:** Encouraging progress and consistency.

**Examples:**

Inner Circle:

Close friends and family you trust completely.

Supportive Acquaintances:

Coworkers, neighbors, and casual friends who can offer specific help.

Professional Networks:

Mentors, coaches, or therapists for expert advice.

Community Groups:

Clubs, volunteer organizations, or online communities that share your values.

## Activity: Mapping Your Support System

| Group Type | Examples | Role in Support System |
|---|---|---|
| Family & Friends | Parents, siblings, best friends | Emotional support, advice, and companionship. |
| Local Communities | Churches, parenting groups, or clubs | Shared experiences and local resources. |
| Professional Contacts | Therapists, mentors, or colleagues | Career guidance, mental health support, or practical advice. |
| Online Networks | Forums, social media groups, or virtual workshops | Access to specialized knowledge and broader perspectives. |

## Organizing Support Groups: Step-by-Step Guide

### 1. Define the Purpose:

- What issue or topic will your group address? (Parenting, grief, addiction recovery, etc.)

- Will it focus on emotional support, resources, or skill-building?

### 2. Choose a Format:

- **In-Person:** Great for deeper connections and activities.

- **Virtual:** Accessible for people in different locations or with busy schedules.

- **Hybrid:** Combines both for flexibility.

### 3. Recruit Members:

- Spread the word through social media, community boards, or word-of-mouth.

- Partner with local organizations for referrals.

### 4. Establish Ground Rules:

- Ensure confidentiality and mutual respect.

- Create guidelines for listening, speaking, and providing feedback.

### 5. Facilitate Meetings:

- Use **icebreakers** to build trust early on.

- Provide discussion prompts to encourage sharing.

- Incorporate activities like **journaling, goal-setting, or group exercises**.

### 6. Maintain Engagement:

- Celebrate milestones, whether personal victories or group anniversaries.

- Provide resources like worksheets, articles, or guest speakers.

### *The Role of Housing*

Beyond emotional connections, physical spaces can also provide the stability needed to grow. Safe and **supportive housing programs** often serve as the backbone for rebuilding lives after setbacks. Whether it's temporary shelters, shared living spaces, or affordable housing programs, these environments offer:

- **Safety:** Removing immediate stressors so individuals can focus on solutions.

- **Community Interaction:** Building connections with others facing similar challenges.

- **Resource Access:** Providing job training, financial planning, and mental health services.

Programs like **transitional housing** and **community co-living** prove that support isn't just emotional—it can also be structural, offering both a roof over one's head and a network of encouragement.

## *YOUR CHECKLIST!*

- o **Host Regular Check-Ins:**

- o **Create a Shared Space:**

- o **Volunteer Together:**

- o **Start a Resource Pool:**

- o **Organize Skill-Building Events:**

**1. Host Regular Check-Ins**

**What It Means:**

Schedule weekly or monthly calls, video chats, or in-person meetings to stay connected with the important people in your life. These check-ins can be casual catch-ups, brainstorming sessions, or opportunities to offer and receive support.

**How to Solve It:**

- **Step 1:** Make a list of the people you want to stay connected with—family, friends, coworkers, or mentors.

- **Step 2:** Set a recurring date on your calendar and invite them in advance to ensure consistency.

- **Step 3:** Use tools like Zoom, Google Meet, or even group messaging apps for easy scheduling and reminders.

- **Step 4:** Keep it structured but informal—share updates, discuss goals, and ask how they're doing to maintain strong bonds.

**Outcome:**

Strengthened relationships and consistent communication will provide emotional support and accountability during challenges.

**2. Create a Shared Space**

**What It Means:**

Establish a space—physical or virtual—where people can gather to share ideas, resources, and experiences.

**How to Solve It:**

- **Step 1:** Find a suitable location, like a library, coffee shop, or community center. If virtual, create a group chat, Slack channel, or Facebook group.

- **Step 2:** Clarify the purpose of the space (e.g., emotional support, shared learning, or project planning).

- **Step 3:** Set ground rules for communication, respect, and participation to create a welcoming atmosphere.

- **Step 4:** Post updates, schedule meetings, and encourage participation to keep the space active and engaging.

**Outcome:**

A safe and inclusive space will encourage collaboration, inspire creativity, and strengthen group ties.

### 3. Volunteer Together

**What It Means:**

Bond with others by working toward a shared cause, whether through charity drives, clean-up campaigns, or community events.

**How to Solve It:**

- **Step 1:** Identify causes that align with your group's interests, such as food drives, environmental cleanups, or mentoring programs.

- **Step 2:** Research local nonprofits or community initiatives and sign up as a group to volunteer.

- **Step 3:** Create a volunteer schedule that fits everyone's availability and share tasks to keep things organized.

- **Step 4:** Reflect on your shared experiences and discuss ways to continue supporting the cause long-term.

**Outcome:**

Volunteering together strengthens relationships, builds purpose, and reinforces teamwork while making a positive impact.

## 4. Start a Resource Pool

**What It Means:**

Create a system where group members can share tools, books, or services to promote collaboration and resourcefulness.

**How to Solve It:**

- **Step 1:** List resources that group members are willing to share—books, office supplies, tools, or expertise.

- **Step 2:** Use a shared spreadsheet or online tool (like Google Sheets) to track who has what and who needs what.

- **Step 3:** Set borrowing rules, such as time limits and care instructions, to ensure fairness and accountability.

- **Step 4:** Rotate responsibility for managing the pool to encourage active participation and organization.

**Outcome:**

Pooling resources reduces waste, lowers costs, and builds a culture of trust and generosity within the group.

## 5. Organize Skill-Building Events

**What It Means:**

Offer free workshops or sessions where participants can learn practical skills like budgeting, resume-building, or parenting tips.

**How to Solve It:**

- **Step 1:** Survey group members to identify skills they want to learn or share.

- **Step 2:** Find speakers, trainers, or volunteers within the group or invite experts from outside the community.

- **Step 3:** Book a venue or set up a virtual meeting link for accessibility.

- **Step 4:** Provide materials or templates in advance, and record sessions to make them available for later use.

- **Step 5:** Follow up with attendees for feedback to improve future workshops.

**Outcome:**

Skill-building events create opportunities for personal growth, strengthen connections, and provide lasting tools for success.

This checklist is more than a to-do list—it's a framework for building stronger, more supportive relationships. Each step creates opportunities for growth, collaboration, and shared success. Whether you start with small check-ins or larger events, the effort you invest in strengthening connections will lead to confidence, stability, and shared momentum for everyone involved.

*Triangle Diagram*

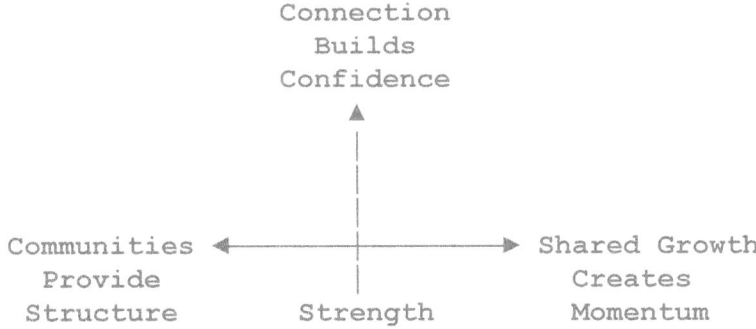

Connection
Builds
Confidence

Communities ← Shared Growth
Provide Creates
Structure     Strength     Momentum

**How It Works:**

✓ The top point represents confidence

✓ The left base symbolizes structure

✓ The right base highlights growth

*Idea:*

The triangle shows how each element supports the others, forming a stable and balanced foundation for personal and emotional growth.

The triangle represents the **interconnected foundation of relationships** and how they contribute to emotional strength and personal growth. At the **top point**, we see **confidence**, which flourishes when we have supportive connections in our lives.

These connections act as anchors, reminding us that we're not alone and giving us the courage to face challenges head-on. Whether it's friends, family, or trusted mentors, these relationships provide

encouragement and reassurance during uncertain times, helping us build belief in ourselves.

Moving to the **left base**, we find **structure**, symbolized by communities and support systems. Just like a house needs a solid foundation to stand firm, people need dependable environments to feel grounded.

Communities—whether they're local groups, faith-based organizations, or online networks—offer stability in moments of uncertainty. They create safe spaces where people can share struggles, exchange ideas, and find resources, turning chaos into order and isolation into belonging.

On the **right base**, we see **growth**, which emerges through accountability, encouragement, and shared progress. Growth is rarely achieved alone—it often happens when we're surrounded by people who push us to be better and celebrate our wins along the way. These relationships keep us motivated, challenge us to stretch beyond our comfort zones, and remind us of how far we've come.

Collected, the three points of the triangle demonstrate how relationships form a **balanced framework** for resilience. Confidence keeps us steady, structure gives us a sense of security, and growth ensures we continue moving forward.

When all three work in harmony, they create a support system that not only helps us withstand life's challenges but also empowers us to thrive.

**Questions:**

1. Who are the people in your life you can count on during difficult times?

   _____

   _____

   _____

   _____

2. What steps can you take this week to strengthen those relationships?

   _____

   _____

   _____

   _____

3. Is there a group or cause you feel connected to that could benefit from your skills or presence?

   _____

   _____

   _____

   _____

*"Strong relationships aren't built by perfect people but by people willing to stand together through imperfect moments."*

# Chapter 12:

# Welcoming the Unknown

*"The unknown isn't the end; it's the awkward start of a story you'll laugh about someday."*

**The Uninvited Houseguest**

Change is like that uninvited houseguest who shows up unannounced, rearranges your furniture, and eats the last slice of pizza. It's disruptive, inconvenient, and leaves you questioning your life choices. But, just like that houseguest, it might actually bring some unexpected joy—or at least a good story to tell later.

The unknown has a knack for arriving when you least expect it, shaking up routines, beliefs, and comfort zones. Sure, it's uncomfortable at first—like squeezing into jeans you haven't worn since college—but it's also an invitation to grow.

**Theoretical Lens: The Growth Zone Model**

The Growth Zone Model divides experiences into three zones:

- **Comfort Zone**: Where routines and predictability dominate.

- **Fear Zone**: The initial reaction to change, marked by discomfort and resistance.

- **Growth Zone**: The stage where adaptation leads to personal development.

When change disrupts the comfort zone, it often throws individuals into the fear zone. The key is how one navigates this space. By facing challenges head-on and reframing the unknown as an opportunity, individuals move into the growth zone, where new skills, perspectives, and resilience emerge.

**Key Insight:**

Resistance to change isn't inherently bad; it's a natural response that, when managed, leads to profound learning.

**2. Academic Perspective: Neuroplasticity and Adaptation**

Neuroscience provides a biological explanation for why the "uninvited houseguest" of change feels so disruptive. The brain is wired to favor established neural pathways—patterns that reflect learned habits and behaviors.

When change occurs, the brain must rewire itself, a process called **neuroplasticity**.

While this rewiring is uncomfortable (and cognitively taxing), it's also how we learn and grow.

For example:

- **The First Reaction**: Initial discomfort arises as the brain struggles to find familiar patterns.

- **Adaptation Phase**: With repeated exposure to new stimuli, the brain strengthens new pathways.

- **Integration**: The new patterns become part of the norm, and what once felt foreign becomes second nature.

**Key Insight:**

Discomfort during change is a sign of the brain's plasticity at work, making way for growth.

## 3. Practical Application: Managing Organizational Change

**Kotter's 8-Step Process** emphasize:

1. Acknowledging the discomfort caused by change (e.g., resistance to new policies or technologies).

2. Communicating the benefits and necessity of the change to reduce fear.

3. Providing support systems (training, feedback, and incentives) to help individuals move from resistance to acceptance.

**Key Insight:**

Change in organizations mirrors personal growth—it's messy but manageable with structure and empathy.

## 4. Philosophical Perspective: Stoicism and the Unknown

Stoic philosophy encourages embracing the unexpected with calm and rationality. Marcus Aurelius wrote, *"You have power over your mind—not outside events. Realize this, and you will find strength."*

In this framework:

- The "uninvited houseguest" symbolizes external events we cannot control.

- Our response represents the realm of agency—how we choose to react and adapt.

**Key Insight:**

The unknown isn't inherently bad; it's our perception of it that determines its impact.

The metaphor of the uninvited houseguest offers a rich platform for understanding change and the human response to it. Whether approached through neuroscience, organizational theory, or philosophy, the takeaway remains consistent: while change disrupts, it also drives growth.

**Losing Your Cool (DON'T)**

When change barges in, the first instinct might be to slam the door shut. Let's face it, we like our comfort zones—they're cozy and predictable, like a favorite pair of sweatpants. But here's the thing: nothing ever grows in a comfort zone except maybe your Netflix watch list.

So, how do you adjust without losing your mind?

1. **Acknowledge Your Feelings (Yes, All of Them):** Feel like screaming into a pillow? Go for it. Denying emotions is like trying to ignore a leaky faucet—it just makes the drip louder.

2. **Break It Down:** Change feels less daunting when you tackle it in small, manageable chunks. Baby steps, not leaps. Unless you're a kangaroo, then by all means, hop.

3. **Stay Curious:** Ask yourself, "What's the worst that could happen? And how likely is that, really?" Spoiler: The odds of spontaneously combusting are pretty low.

4. **Find Your Cheerleaders:** Surround yourself with people who remind you that you've survived every awkward moment so far—including middle school.

## Channeling Your Inner Sponge

Receptiveness isn't about loving change; it's about tolerating it long enough to see the upside. Think of it like eating kale—not great at first, but surprisingly beneficial once you get used to it.

How to hug the chaos?

- **Stay Mindful:** Instead of spiraling into a "worst-case scenario" montage, take a moment to breathe. Deep breaths, not hyperventilation—there's a difference.

- **Reframe the Challenge:** Imagine change is a workout for your brain. Sure, it's uncomfortable, but hey, it's making you mentally ripped.

- **Celebrate Tiny Wins:** Managed to figure out one small part of the new software? Throw yourself a mini dance party (or at least a fist pump).

**Activities for Growth** *(Now With Extra Fun)*

- **Reflection Exercise:** Write about the last time change turned out better than expected. If you can't think of anything, reflect on how you survived the time your favorite coffee shop ran out of oat milk.

- **Gratitude Practice:** Jot down three unexpected perks from a recent challenge. Even "I learned to function on three hours of sleep" counts.

- **Visualization:** Close your eyes and picture yourself mastering this change like a pro. Bonus points if you imagine a cape fluttering behind you.

Greeting the unknown is like opening a mystery box. Sure, it could be socks, but it could also be a puppy. The trick is to open it anyway and see what's inside.

**Unpredictable Umbrella**

Life's surprises often come unannounced, shaking the foundation of our routines and plans. Yet, humor acts as a remarkable coping mechanism in these moments, offering perspective and relief. Psychologists emphasize that laughter isn't just a distraction; it rewires how we perceive challenges, helping to reduce stress and improve resilience. When we approach life with humor, even the most daunting uncertainties can feel less overwhelming, allowing us to navigate them with greater ease.

Existentialist philosophers suggest that the unknown is not a threat but a realm of possibility. Kierkegaard's idea of the "leap of faith" reflects the importance of trusting the process, even when outcomes are uncertain. This trust transforms fear into freedom, enabling us to explore paths we might otherwise avoid. Trusting the process, then, becomes not only an act of courage but also a commitment to self-discovery.

**The Biology of Adaptation**

From an evolutionary perspective, the ability to adapt to unexpected changes is essential for growth and survival. The brain's plasticity allows us to reframe stress as an opportunity to learn and evolve. Just as species thrive by adjusting to shifting environments, individuals can flourish by leaning into life's surprises, turning discomfort into strength.

In the professional world, uncertainty often leads to innovation. Agile methodologies, widely adopted in industries like technology, embrace surprises as opportunities for improvement. Leaders who trust the process and maintain a sense of humor during challenges create resilient teams that excel under pressure. This principle applies beyond business—adopting a flexible mindset and staying open to unexpected outcomes can lead to transformative personal growth.

**Joseph Campbell's *Hero***

*The Journey* reminds us that growth begins when we step into the unknown. The challenges we face are not mere obstacles but pivotal moments that shape our character. Along the way, unexpected allies and opportunities emerge, reminding us that the adventure is as much about the journey as the destination. When we lean into life's surprises with humor and trust, we find opportunities to redefine ourselves.

# Chapter 13:

# The Mindset Shift

*"It's not the mountain we conquer but ourselves."* – Sir Edmund Hillary

When life gets tough, the difference between staying stuck and moving forward often comes down to mindset.

By transforming how we perceive difficulties—viewing them as challenges rather than insurmountable obstacles—we unlock the potential for growth.

This chapter explores how to develop a growth-oriented mindset, back beliefs with action, and embrace challenges as stepping stones to success.

*"The greatest glory in living lies not in never falling, but in rising every time we fall."* – Nelson Mandela

**Reframing Difficulties as Challenges**

Our thoughts shape our reality. The way we interpret a situation determines how we respond to it. Consider the difference between these two mindsets:

| Fixed Mindset | Growth Mindset |
| --- | --- |
| "I can't do this; it's too hard." | "This is tough, but I can learn from it." |

| Fixed Mindset | Growth Mindset |
|---|---|
| "Failure defines me." | "Failure teaches me." |
| "I'm just not good at this." | "I can improve with effort." |

**Dialogue Examples**:

**Alex:** *"I failed my presentation. I'm terrible at public speaking."*

**Jordan:** *"Or maybe it's a skill you haven't mastered yet. What did you learn for next time?"*

**Grip the Process Over the Outcome**

Success isn't about the finish line—it's about the journey. Shift focus from results to effort, and growth will naturally follow.

**Quote:** "Success is the sum of small efforts, repeated day in and day out." – Robert Collier

**Activity:**

Write down three ways you've improved in an area where you once struggled.

_____

_____

_____

_____

_____

_____

_____

## Turn Setbacks Into Opportunities

## Table: Transforming Setbacks into Lessons

| Setback | Emotion | Lesson Learned | Next Action |
|---|---|---|---|
| Missed a project deadline | Frustration | Poor time management | Create a detailed schedule |
| Failed a certification exam | Disappointment | Need to study differently | Try practice tests and revision plans |

This table breaks down how setbacks can teach us valuable lessons and guide us toward improving in the future. It shows a simple way to process challenges by focusing on what went wrong, how it made you feel, what you can learn, and what to do next.

**Missed a project deadline**:

- o **Emotion**: Frustration—you feel upset or annoyed because you didn't meet the deadline.

- o **Lesson Learned**: Poor time management—you realize you didn't plan or prioritize your time well.

- o **Next Action**: Create a detailed schedule—by organizing your tasks and deadlines, you can manage your time better next time.

**_OR_ Failed a certification exam**:

- o **Emotion**: Disappointment—you feel let down or sad because you didn't pass.

- o **Lesson Learned**: Need to study differently—your current study methods aren't effective, so you need a new approach.

○ **Next Action**: Try practice tests and revision plans—by using tools like mock exams or revising specific topics, you can prepare more effectively and improve your chances of passing.

This table reminds us that setbacks are not failures but opportunities to learn and grow by taking actionable steps. By analyzing what went wrong, you gain insights that help you succeed next time.

**Surround Yourself with Growth-Oriented People**

**Emma:** *"I'm thinking of trying for a promotion, but I'm scared I won't make it."*

**Liam:** *"The only way to know is to try. Even if you don't get it, you'll learn something valuable."*

This dialogue illustrates the importance of taking risks and adopting a growth mindset when facing challenges. Here's a simple explanation:

- **Emma's Perspective**: She is considering going for a promotion but feels scared because she doubts her ability to succeed. Her fear of failure is holding her back from taking action.

- **Liam's Advice**: He encourages Emma to try despite her fear. He emphasizes that even if she doesn't succeed, the experience itself will be valuable. She'll learn from the process—whether it's gaining insights about her strengths, understanding what she needs to improve, or building confidence for future opportunities.

**Key Takeaway**: The conversation highlights that taking action, even when success isn't guaranteed, is a crucial step toward personal growth. Failure is not the end—it's part of the journey to learning and improving.

*The company you keep influences your mindset. Surround yourself with people who inspire you to challenge yourself.*

**Backing with Action**

Beliefs without action are like seeds without water—they hold potential but never grow.

Here's how to put your growth mindset into practice:

**1. Set SMART Goals**

Create Specific, Measurable, Achievable, Relevant, and Time-bound goals to turn intentions into actionable steps.

**Example Goal**:

*"I will improve my public speaking by practicing with a small group once a week for the next three months."*

### Track Your Progress

| Day | Task Completed | Lesson Learned | Next Step |
|---|---|---|---|
| Monday | Practiced a speech | Need to slow down my delivery | Focus on pacing next session |
| Thursday | Got feedback from peers | Eye contact is critical | Practice engaging with the audience |

**Visualizing…**

*CHART:*

*Growth Mindset in Action*

- **Stage 1: Awareness**

  Realize limiting beliefs.

- **Stage 2: Reframing**

  Replace negative thoughts with positive, action-oriented ones.

- **Stage 3: Execution**

  Act on beliefs with clear, consistent steps.

- **Stage 4: Reflection**

  Analyze outcomes and refine strategies.

*"You miss 100% of the shots you don't take."* – Wayne Gretzky

### Mia's Mindset

**Before:** Mia avoided leadership roles because she feared failure.

**Trigger Event:** Her manager asked her to lead a small team project.

**Mindset Shift:** With encouragement from her peers, Mia reframed the opportunity as a chance to learn.

**Actions:**

- Attended leadership workshops.

- Sought feedback regularly.

**Result:** The project succeeded, and Mia gained the confidence to pursue bigger opportunities.

The mindset shift from seeing difficulties as obstacles to viewing them as challenges requires consistent effort but yields immense rewards. By reframing your perspective, surrounding yourself with positive influences, and backing beliefs with action, you create a cycle of growth that transforms not only your mindset but also your life.

*"Every challenge is a stepping stone. It's up to you to climb."*

# Chapter 14:

# The Everyday Resilience

*"Strength doesn't come from what you can do; it comes from overcoming the things you once thought you couldn't."* — Rikki Rogers

**One Day at a Time**

Resilience doesn't require a superhero cape or a standing ovation—it's hidden in the little things we do daily. It's waking up after a lousy night's sleep and still managing to laugh at your coffee spilling because, really, what's one more thing? It's the quiet persistence of picking up where you left off, even when life feels like it's on shuffle mode with no "next" button in sight.

Handling the unexpected isn't about grand gestures; it's about the steady grind of showing up. Whether it's tackling a deadline while the Wi-Fi decides to go on strike or smiling at a stranger when your patience is paper-thin, these tiny victories are what keep us moving forward.

Recovering from life's curveballs doesn't have to look graceful—it's about staying on your feet, even if you're wobbling a little. Maybe you've had a bad day, but hey, if you've managed to find humor in a burnt dinner or a broken shoelace, that's resilience in action.

One day at a time isn't just advice—it's a strategy. It's about giving yourself the grace to handle what you can, letting the rest go, and finding strength in the fact that you're still standing (or at least sitting upright).

**Table: Micro-Resilience Practices**

| Practice | Action | Benefit |
|---|---|---|
| Morning Routine | Begin each day with a calming ritual, like journaling or stretching. | Sets a positive tone for the day. |
| Gratitude Moments | Write down 3 things you're thankful for each evening. | Shifts focus from stress to positivity. |
| Deep Breathing | Take 3 deep breaths during moments of stress. | Reduces anxiety and improves focus. |
| Hydration Breaks | Drink water regularly and mindfully. | Boosts energy and mental clarity. |
| Disconnecting from Screens | Spend 30 minutes offline daily. | Restores mental balance and reduces fatigue. |

*"Resilience is about building habits that sustain us, not waiting for the storm to pass."*

**Everyday Checklists**

A structured checklist can help maintain focus and track progress. Start your day by selecting three items from the checklist and commit to completing them.

**Examples**

1. Drink a glass of water as soon as you wake up.

2. Write down one thing you're grateful for today.

3. Take a 10-minute walk or stretch.

4. Respond to one email or message you've been putting off.

5. Read one page of a book or an article that inspires you.

6. Organize your workspace for 5 minutes.

7. Compliment someone genuinely.

8. Set a small goal for the day and write it down.

9. Take three deep breaths to center yourself.

10. Spend five minutes reviewing or planning your schedule.

**Reflection Prompt**:

After completing your three items, ask yourslf:

- *Did this help me feel more productive, relaxed, or motivated?*

- *What would I like to carry forward tomorrow?*

**Activity:** Reflect on how they make you feel.

_____

_____

_____

_____

_____

_____

_____

## Conversations That Strengthen

Resilience often grows through connection. Conversations can offer perspective, support, and encouragement.

### Examples of Dialogues in Different Relationships:

1. **Parent and Child**

   o Parent: "I know you're upset about your grade, but let's talk about what you can do differently next time. I believe in you."

   o Child: "Thanks, Mom. I think I need to manage my study time better."

2. **Friends**

   o Friend 1: "I'm feeling stuck at work. It's like I'm going nowhere."

   o Friend 2: "I get that. But remember when you felt this way about your last project? You ended up nailing it. What's one thing you could try now?"

3. **Mentor and Mentee**

   o Mentee: "I made a mistake at work, and now I feel like I've ruined everything."

   o Mentor: "Everyone makes mistakes—it's how you handle them that matters. Let's brainstorm how you can fix it and what you'll do differently next time."

## 4. Partners

- Partner 1: "This week has been exhausting. I feel like I can't catch a break."

- Partner 2: "I'm sorry it's been so tough. Let's take a walk tonight and talk about what's been weighing on you."

## 5. Teacher and Student

- Student: "I'm struggling with this topic. I don't think I'll ever get it."

- Teacher: "You've made progress before, and you will again. Let's break it down together—it's okay to need help."

## 6. Colleagues

- Colleague 1: "The client hated my idea. I'm questioning if I'm even good at this job."

- Colleague 2: "That's rough, but one idea doesn't define you. Let's refine it and try again. You've got this."

## Key Takeaway:

Each of these conversations emphasizes encouragement, and constructive feedback. The relationships we foster through meaningful dialogue remind us that we're never truly facing challenges alone.

### The Resilience Cycle

| 1.  Event |
| --- |
| 2.  Emotion |
| 3.  Reframe |
| 4.  Action |
| 5.  Growth |

☐ Acknowledge **the Setback**

- Accept what happened without judgment. Recognize your emotions and give yourself space to process them.

☐ Reframe **the Situation**

- Shift your mindset to see the setback as a learning opportunity rather than a failure. Ask, "What can I learn from this?"

☐ Set **Realistic Goals**

- Break your recovery into smaller, achievable steps. Focus on immediate, actionable tasks that bring you closer to your larger goal.

☐ Develop **a Plan**

- Identify what went wrong and create a detailed plan to address the issue. Use SMART goals to stay focused.

☐ Practice **Self-Compassion**

- Treat yourself with kindness. Avoid self-criticism and remind yourself that setbacks are part of growth.

☐ Seek **Support**

- Lean on friends, family, or mentors for guidance, encouragement, and perspective. Don't hesitate to ask for help.

☐ Focus **on Strengths**

- Reflect on past successes and use your strengths to tackle current challenges. Build confidence from what you've already overcome.

☐ Take **Care of Your Well-Being**

- Prioritize self-care through proper sleep, nutrition, and exercise. A healthy body supports a resilient mind.

☐ Stay **Flexible**

- Be willing to adapt and try new approaches if the original plan isn't working. Flexibility is key to resilience.

☐ Celebrate **Progress**

- Acknowledge small victories along the way. Each step forward, no matter how minor, is a sign of progress.

☐ Learn **and Apply Lessons**

- Reflect on the experience and integrate the lessons into your approach. Use setbacks to refine your strategies for the future.

☐ Maintain **Optimism**

- Focus on the possibilities ahead. A positive outlook fuels resilience and motivates action.

☐ Visualize **Success**

- Picture yourself overcoming the challenge. Visualization reinforces belief in your ability to succeed.

☐ Take **Action**

- Start small, but start. Even incremental actions build momentum and restore a sense of control.

☐ Be **Patient**

- *Understand that bouncing back takes time. Be consistent!*

**Example:** If you're turned down for a job, reframe it as an opportunity to refine your interview skills and target better-suited positions.

**The ABC Method**

- **A**: **Adversity** — Identify the challenge.

- **B**: **Belief** — Examine your thoughts about it.

- **C**: **Consequence** — Consider how those beliefs affect your actions.

The ABC Method is a simple yet powerful tool for understanding and managing our reactions to challenges. Developed by Dr. Albert Ellis as part of Rational Emotive Behavior Therapy (REBT), this approach helps us dissect how our beliefs about adversity influence our emotional and behavioral responses. By breaking situations down into three parts:

A: Adversity – Identify the Challenge

The first step is recognizing the specific event or situation causing stress or difficulty. Adversity could range from missing a deadline at work to facing a personal setback, like a relationship breakdown. By clearly identifying the challenge, you gain clarity on what you're dealing with.

Example:

**Adversity: You didn't get the promotion you were hoping for.**

B: Belief – Examine Your Thoughts About It

Next, reflect on the beliefs you hold about the situation. Are they rational and grounded, or are they shaped by fear, self-doubt, or pessimism? Beliefs are often the linchpin in determining whether we react constructively or destructively.

Example:

**Belief: "I'm not enough for the promotion. I'll never advance in my career."**

By identifying limiting beliefs, you can challenge them and replace them with empowering alternatives.

C: Consequence – Consider How Beliefs Affect Your Actions

Finally, analyze the consequences of holding these beliefs. How do they impact your emotions and behavior? Negative beliefs often lead to feelings of frustration, discouragement, or even avoidance of future opportunities. Constructive beliefs, on the other hand, foster growth and motivation.

Example:

**Consequence: Believing you're "not good enough" leads to self-doubt, reducing your confidence and discouraging you from applying for future promotions.**

**Rewriting the Narrative**

By revisiting the belief stage and reframing it, you can change the outcome.

Revised Belief:

**"This promotion wasn't the right fit, but I can use this as feedback to grow and prepare for the next opportunity."**

Revised Consequence:

**With a growth-oriented belief, you feel motivated to seek feedback, enhance your skills, and apply for other roles, ultimately leading to progress.**

*Takeaway*

**The ABC Method** empowers us to take control of our thoughts and actions, transforming adversity into a catalyst for growth so we can break free from negative cycles.

> *"Adversity doesn't define us—our response does."*

**Activity:**

Write down an adversity you're facing and use the ABC method to shift your perspective.

_____

_____

_____

_____

_____

_____

_____

_____

Building everyday resilience is about small, consistent actions. By integrating micro-practices, maintaining supportive conversations, and using practical tools, you're not just preparing for life's challenges—you're growing stronger every day.

# Chapter 15:

# Stories of Hope and Resilience

*"Hope is being able to see that there is light despite all of the darkness."* — Desmond Tutu

**Learning from Others**

The stories of those who have experiences and overcome adversity serve as invaluable lessons for us all. These stories act as guiding lights, showing us what is possible when determination meets courage. They retell us that we are not alone in our struggles and that resilience is a skill we can learn from others.

By listening to their journeys, we can:

1. **Find Inspiration**: Seeing someone rise above challenges can ignite hope in our own lives.

2. **Learn Strategies**: Their successes and failures offer practical insights into overcoming obstacles.

3. **Build Connection**: Shared stories create a sense of community, reassuring us that others understand and have walked similar paths.

Whether through biographies, documentaries, or conversations with loved ones, learning from others' resilience equips us with tools and

motivation to navigate our own hardships. Their strength becomes a blueprint for our growth.

1. **Nelson Mandela**

   - **Challenge**: Imprisoned for 27 years under apartheid.

   - **Resilience**: Maintained hope, learned patience, and emerged as a unifying leader.

   - **Takeaway**: "It always seems impossible until it's done." Mandela's ability to stay focused on his vision of equality demonstrates the power of hope during hardship.

2. **Mia's Small Business**

   - **Struggle**: Lost her job during the pandemic.

   - **Action**: Turned her baking hobby into a thriving online business.

   - **Lesson**: Resilience often starts with taking small steps toward a new direction.

**Mia:** *"I never thought I'd run a business, but losing my job forced me to try."*

**Friend:** *"And look at you now! That risk turned into a reward."*

## 3. Key Elements

| Element | Description | Example |
|---|---|---|
| Vision | A clear goal or purpose. | Mandela's dream of a free South Africa. |
| Perseverance | The ability to keep going. | Scientists who failed repeatedly before success. |
| Support Systems | Help from others. | Communities rallying during natural disasters. |
| Growth Through Pain | Lessons learned from struggles. | Turning personal loss into advocacy. |

## 4. The Wright Brothers

- Wilbur and Orville Wright grew up fascinated by the idea of human flight, inspired by kites and bird movements.

- They dreamed of a machine that could carry humans through the air.

- **1900-1902**: The brothers tested unpowered gliders on the windy dunes of Kitty Hawk, North Carolina.

  o **Setback**: Many crashes and design failures.

  o **Lesson Learned**: They realized they needed better control mechanisms and understanding of aerodynamics.

- They meticulously collected data from their test flights, challenging established aviation theories.

- Built a homemade wind tunnel to refine their designs—a groundbreaking approach at the time.

- **December 17, 1903**: On a cold morning in Kitty Hawk, the Wright Flyer lifted off the ground, staying airborne for 12 seconds.

  o This was humanity's first powered, sustained, and controlled flight.

  o **Significance**: Years of persistence culminated in a historic moment.

- The Wright Brothers continued to improve their designs, inspiring the aviation industry.

- Their invention paved the way for modern air travel.

  - **Challenge**: Multiple failed attempts at flight.

  - **Resilience**: Innovation led to the first powered flight.

  - **Lesson**: Failure is often groundbreaking success.

**Modern Example:** *Malala Yousafzai*

On an ordinary morning in 2012, a school bus wound its way through the Swat Valley in Pakistan. Among the students was a 15-year-old girl named Malala Yousafzai. Like her classmates, she carried books and dreams, but she also carried something far more dangerous: a bold belief that every girl deserved the right to an education.

For years, Malala had been outspoken about the growing restrictions imposed by the Taliban, who sought to silence the voices of women and girls in her region. Her activism had already gained attention, but it also drew unwanted scrutiny from those who opposed her cause.

That morning, Malala's world changed forever. A masked man boarded the bus, called her by name, and fired a bullet that struck her head. The news of the assassination attempt sent shockwaves around the globe. Malala's survival was uncertain, and the future of her advocacy seemed grim.

But Malala herself is unshakable.

After months of intensive medical treatment in the United Kingdom, Malala defied the odds. She not only recovered but returned stronger than ever, her voice amplified by the global platform that emerged from her tragedy. Instead of retreating in fear, Malala chose to stand even taller, transforming her personal ordeal into a mission to uplift others.

She co-founded the Malala Fund, an organization dedicated to championing education for girls worldwide. She addressed the United Nations, sharing her story and calling for action. Her message was clear: "One child, one teacher, one book, and one pen can change the world."

*"They thought the bullets would silence me, but they failed. Out of that silence came thousands of voices."* – Malala Yousafzai

**Resilience**: Became a global advocate for education and equality.

**Lesson**: Courage can inspire change on a global scale.

Malala's story became hope, illustrating the power to ripple far beyond individual struggles.

Her journey, from the trauma of an assassination attempt to becoming the youngest-ever Nobel Peace Prize laureate, inspired millions to believe in the transformative power of education and equality.

The lesson is profound: adversity can try to silence a voice, but resilience ensures it is heard louder than ever.

Through her strength, Malala taught the world that one person's courage can ignite change on a global scale.

Her story reminds us that when faced with insurmountable challenges, choosing to persist can not only reshape our lives but also transform the lives of others.

**Activity:**

**Write Your Own Resilience Story**

1. Reflect on a time you overcame a challenge.

_____

_____

_____

_____

_____

_____

_____

_____

2. Identify what helped you persevere.

_____

_____

_____

_____

_____

_____

_____

_____

_____

_____

3. Share your story with a friend. **Done? Yes or No**

_____

**Prompt:** *Exploring Historical Resilience*

Research a historical figure who faced adversity. Who did you choose?

_____

What lessons can you apply to your life?

_____

_____

_____

_____

_____

_____

_____

_____

_____

_____

_____

_____

_____

_____

_____

**TAKEAWAYS:**

a) **Resilience is Universal**

b) **Hope Fuels Strength**

c) **Sharing Stories Matters**

Here's a chart that explains the above takeaways visually:

| Explanation | Example | Key Message |
|---|---|---|
| Resilience is a human quality found across cultures and eras, showing that overcoming hardship is part of the human experience. | Ancient stories of survival like Odysseus in *The Odyssey* or real-life figures like Malala Yousafzai. | Resilience is not bound by time or place; it's a shared human trait. |
| Having a purpose and belief in a better future gives people the motivation to endure and persevere. | Viktor Frankl survived the Holocaust by focusing on the meaning of life, captured in *Man's Search for Meaning*. | A clear vision and hope provide the mental strength needed to navigate tough situations. |
| Hearing or reading stories of resilience helps individuals feel less alone and inspires strength in others. | Personal testimonies of recovery from illness or interviews with war survivors inspire action. | Stories of resilience remind us that others have faced and overcome similar struggles. |

# Chapter 16:

# Pledging Allegiance to the Resilience Work

*"Resilience isn't just about surviving—it's about creating strength that lifts others as we rise."*

Resilience is more than just bouncing back from challenges; it's about thriving in the face of adversity. It grows through deliberate personal effort and a collective commitment to uplift ourselves and those around us. It's a quiet promise, a dedication to spread strength—not only for personal benefit but for the well-being of our communities. When we intentionally nurture resilience both personally and collectively, we transform challenges into opportunities for growth and connection.

**The Dual Mission:**

The dual mission refers to the interconnected effort of developing personal resilience while fostering collective strength within a community. It highlights the need for both individual self-improvement and collaborative action to create a holistic framework for thriving in the face of challenges.

*Key Idea: The dual mission emphasizes that resilience is not an isolated endeavor. By balancing self-care with collective well-being, the dual mission fosters a cycle of continuous growth.*

## 1. Start Within: Personal Resilience

Resilience begins with the individual. It's the result of self-awareness, reflection, and the decision to see struggles as opportunities for growth. This involves focusing on oneself—cultivating habits, skills, and mindsets that enhance emotional, mental, and physical well-being. Practices empower individuals to face adversity with confidence and adaptability. Developing resilience requires consistent effort and a willingness to adapt to life's unpredictability.

**Action Plan**:

### 1. Reflection Journal:

Spend at least 10 minutes daily reflecting on your emotional highs and lows. Identify lessons from the day, and consider how you responded to challenges. Over time, this practice creates a roadmap of your growth.

### 2. Visualization Exercises:

Close your eyes and imagine yourself successfully overcoming a current challenge. Picture the steps you'll take and the satisfaction of succeeding. Visualization builds confidence and a proactive mindset.

### 3. Habit-Building:

Start small by incorporating micro-practices into your day. These can include gratitude journaling, practicing mindfulness, or setting SMART goals (Specific, Measurable, Achievable, Relevant, and Time-bound) to stay focused and motivated.

**Example**:

• Reflection:

*"I was frustrated at work today. Why? I didn't feel prepared for a meeting."*

• Visualization:

*"Next time, I'll take 10 minutes beforehand to review my points and anticipate questions."*

• Action:

Create a checklist to prepare for meetings moving forward.

_____

_____

_____

_____

_____

_____

_____

_____

_____

## 2. Extending Beyond: Mobilizing Others

Resilience reaches its full potential when it's shared. Supporting others in their struggles creates a ripple effect, spreading positivity and strength throughout communities. This focuses on building a network of mutual encouragement and shared resources. Collaborative efforts help toughen the joint ability to respond to difficulties.

**Strategies for Community Resilience**:

1. **Storytelling Workshops**:

   Stories connect us. Organize spaces where individuals can share personal narratives of resilience. These workshops create a sense of belonging, inspire hope, and remind participants that they are not alone in their struggles.

2. **Skill-Building Initiatives**:

   Empower people by teaching practical skills like financial literacy, communication, or conflict resolution. These abilities not only build individual confidence but also strengthen the community as a whole.

3. **Community Challenges**:

   Create shared goals, such as completing a neighborhood cleanup, organizing a wellness event, or starting a mentoring program. These activities build teamwork and collective pride.

Resilience can be cultivated both individually and collectively, with each approach complementing the other.

Here's a breakdown of how personal and community efforts work together to foster emotional strength, skill-building, and goal achievement:

**Table: Individual vs. Community Actions**

|  | **Individual Effort** | **Community Action** |
| --- | --- | --- |
| **Emotional Support** | Journaling, mindfulness | Hosting support circles or safe spaces |
| **Skill Development** | Taking courses, learning tools | Organizing workshops or seminars |
| **Goal Setting** | Setting personal SMART goals | Establishing collective, measurable goals |

**Mobilizing Resilience: The Power of Conversations**

Conversations are one of the simplest yet most impactful ways to strengthen resilience in others. A thoughtful word or shared perspective can inspire someone to see a challenge differently or rekindle their hope.

**Examples of Strengthening Dialogue**:

1. **Parent and Teen**:

   o **Parent**: *"I know this year has been tough, but each challenge is shaping you into someone stronger."*

   o **Teen**: *"It doesn't feel like it now, but I'll try to see it that way."*

2. **Community Leader and Volunteer**:

   o **Leader**: *"This initiative could change lives. How can we use our strengths to make it happen?"*

   o **Volunteer**: *"Let's start by listing actionable steps for everyone."*

Supportive and constructive conversations play a critical role in fostering resilience by offering hope, guidance, and actionable strategies. Through thoughtful dialogue, individuals are encouraged to view challenges as opportunities for growth and take steps to move forward.

In the case of a parent and teen, the parent acknowledges the teen's struggles while reframing them as opportunities for personal development. This approach emphasizes long-term benefits, providing reassurance and encouragement. Although the teen may not immediately recognize the value of their experiences, the parent's empathetic and forward-thinking perspective plants the seed of resilience, helping the teen view adversity as a stepping stone rather than a setback.

Similarly, in a dialogue between a community leader and volunteer, the leader highlights the potential impact of an initiative and fosters collaboration by seeking input. This inclusive approach creates a sense of shared responsibility and purpose. The volunteer, motivated by the leader's encouragement, responds with actionable steps, transforming abstract ideas into concrete plans. This exchange not only strengthens teamwork but also reinforces a collective sense of accomplishment.

Both examples demonstrate how meaningful conversations validate feelings, reframe challenges into opportunities, and encourage collaboration. Acknowledging perspectives builds trust and understanding, while focusing on actionable steps empowers individuals to move forward with confidence. These dialogues illustrate that resilience is not built in isolation but through thoughtful communication that inspires individuals and communities to overcome obstacles and grow.

**Interactive Prompt**:

Imagine a friend is feeling hopeless about a situation. Write a short script for a conversation that could inspire them to see things differently. Practice delivering the conversation to ensure it feels natural and encouraging.

_____

_____

_____

_____

_____

_____

_____

_____

_____

_____

_____

_____

**Practical Tools for Resilience**

To make resilience a daily practice, it's helpful to use specific tools and frameworks that provide clarity and structure.

**1. Community Resilience Map**

- Identify the resources, safe spaces, and supportive individuals in your community.

- Use the map to visualize how these elements can collaborate to create a stronger, more connected support network.

A **Community Resilience Map** is a practical tool designed to identify and harness the strengths within your community to create a supportive and connected network. By highlighting available resources, safe spaces, and key individuals who contribute to the well-being of the community, this map serves as a guide to foster resilience collectively.

**Step 1: Identify Resources**

Start by listing the tangible and intangible resources available within your community. These might include:

- Local organizations or non-profits offering services like counseling, food distribution, or job assistance.

- Educational institutions providing access to learning or skill-building programs.

- Healthcare facilities for physical and mental health support.

**Example**:

- The local library offers free workshops on financial literacy.

- A nearby clinic hosts weekly mental health support groups.

## Step 2: Locate Safe Spaces

Identify spaces where people feel welcome, secure, and comfortable. These could be:

- Community centers or recreational areas.

- Religious institutions or places of worship.

- Parks or shared public spaces conducive to relaxation and connection.

**Example**:

- A community park with open seating for casual gatherings.

- A neighborhood café that hosts open-mic nights, fostering connections.

## Step 3: Recognize Supportive Individuals

Pinpoint key people in the community who inspire, lead, or provide support. These might include:

- Teachers, mentors, or social workers.

- Local business owners who contribute to community well-being.

- Informal leaders who organize events or advocate for communal interests.

**Example**:

- A retired teacher who offers free tutoring sessions for kids.

- A local activist organizing clean-up drives and awareness campaigns.

**Step 4: Visualize Collaboration**

Use the map to identify how these resources, spaces, and individuals can work together to strengthen the community. For instance:

- Hosting a health fair at a community center, combining healthcare resources with volunteer support.

- Organizing skill-building workshops in a safe, accessible space like a library or park.

**Outcome**

A Community Resilience Map helps you understand what's available, reveals opportunities for collaboration, and provides a clear visual representation of how interconnected resources and people can come to create a stronger support network for everyone involved.

**2. Action Pyramid**

- **Base Level**: Build personal habits such as mindfulness, gratitude, and journaling.

- **Middle Level**: Participate in shared activities like volunteering or attending community workshops.

- **Top Level**: Take on leadership roles such as mentoring others or organizing events.

The above **Action Pyramid** outlines a step-by-step approach to building resilience, starting with individual habits and expanding to community involvement and leadership. At the **base level**, personal habits like practicing mindfulness, maintaining a gratitude journal, or reflecting daily through journaling help establish a strong foundation for mental and emotional well-being. These habits foster self-awareness and emotional regulation, which are essential for handling challenges. Moving to the **middle level**, engaging in shared activities such as volunteering, attending community workshops, or joining support groups strengthens social connections and creates a sense of belonging. These activities not only enhance personal growth but also contribute to the collective well-being of the community. At the **top level**, taking on leadership roles like mentoring others, organizing events, or spearheading initiatives amplifies the ripple effect of resilience. Leaders inspire others by sharing their knowledge and fostering collaboration, ultimately creating a network of strength and positivity. The pyramid illustrates how resilience grows progressively, beginning with self-care and expanding outward to influence and uplift others.

**Examples in Action**

1. **Personal Story**:

   o   Sarah, a teacher, faced burnout after a particularly challenging school year. She started a daily gratitude journal and began attending local educator meet-ups. Sharing experiences with peers reminded her that she wasn't alone, and together, they developed strategies to make the workload more manageable.

2. **Community Effort**:

   o   In a small town recovering from a flood, residents came together to clean debris, rebuild homes, and support affected families. One volunteer started a daily coordination group, ensuring everyone had clear tasks and a sense of purpose. This collective resilience not only restored the town but strengthened relationships among its residents.

Resilience is an active process that requires consistent effort and a conscious decision to grow stronger through challenges. It isn't something we can develop by staying in our comfort zones.

Research shows that resilience is built through intentional actions, such as setting goals, cultivating a positive mindset, and seeking support from others.

Studies by the American Psychological Association suggest that people who actively work on their emotional and mental strength are more likely to recover from setbacks and thrive during adversity.

Building resilience involves a mix of self-care and outward support. On a personal level, practicing habits like journaling, mindfulness, or regular exercise strengthens mental well-being and prepares us for unexpected challenges.

According to a study published in *Psychological Science*, people who maintain a gratitude practice experience higher levels of optimism, which is a critical component of resilience.

Beyond personal growth, resilience thrives in community. Supporting others through shared experiences or collective goals helps build a network of strength and encouragement.

Research from Harvard University highlights that strong social connections improve not only emotional health but also the ability to bounce back from life's difficulties. By engaging with others—whether through mentorship, group activities, or simply listening—we create a ripple effect of positivity that enhances resilience for everyone involved.

Ultimately, pliability is a skill that develops over time with practice and commitment. It's about turning obstacles into opportunities, finding strength in adversity, and helping others do the same. By building this quality in our communities, we create a lasting foundation of possibility.

**Reflection Question:**

What is one actionable step you can take today to inspire resilience in someone else?

_____

_____

_____

_____

_____

_____

**Small-Scale Community Efforts**

## 1. Crowdfunding as a Catalyst for Change

In recent years, crowdfunding platforms like GoFundMe, Kickstarter, and Indiegogo have become modern tools for resilience.

These platforms allow individuals and communities to pool resources and address pressing needs, often with remarkable outcomes.

### Case Study: A Small Bakery Saves a Town

- **Challenge**: A small bakery in a flood-hit town faced closure, threatening jobs and access to affordable food.

- **Action**: The bakery owner launched a crowdfunding campaign, setting a modest goal of $5,000 to repair equipment and restock supplies.

- **Outcome**: The campaign went viral, raising $50,000. Not only was the bakery saved, but surplus funds were used to provide free meals to displaced families and support local farmers.

**Insight**: Crowdfunding empowers communities by turning collective generosity into tangible impact. A single small-scale initiative can ripple out, benefiting far more people than originally intended.

## 2. Grassroots Movements and Their Ripple Effect

Grassroots organizations often tackle challenges that larger institutions overlook, focusing on hyper-local issues with innovative solutions.

**Example: Neighborhood Garden Revitalization**

- **Problem**: A neglected urban park became a hotspot for crime.

- **Solution**: A group of neighbors pooled resources to clean the area, plant gardens, and install lighting.

- **Impact**: The crime rate dropped by 30%, and the park became a hub for community events, boosting local morale and fostering connections.

*Chart: Elements of Successful Grassroots Movements*

| *Examples:* | | |
|---|---|---|
| **Community Buy-In** | Engaging local stakeholders for support | Neighbors contributing labor |
| **Modest Goals** | Starting small to build momentum | Cleaning one section of the park |
| **Sustainability** | Ensuring long-term impact through maintenance plans | Rotating responsibility for upkeep |

## Reinvention and Overcoming Obstacles

### From Loss to Legacy: Reinventing Careers

Adversity often forces individuals to rethink their paths, leading to remarkable reinventions.

### Profile: The Photographer Who Became a Chef

- **Background**: Mia, a professional photographer, lost her job during the pandemic.

- **Turning Point**: Inspired by her late grandmother's recipes, she began cooking for friends and sharing the process online.

- **Outcome**: What started as a small hobby turned into a thriving catering business, winning awards and creating a legacy inspired by family traditions.

*Key Message:* Reinvention often begins with a small step—exploring a passion, embracing change, or adapting skills in new ways.

### Overcoming Unconventional Obstacles

Some individuals face unique challenges that require extraordinary resilience.

### Example: Through Disability

- **Story**: David, a former athlete, lost his mobility in an accident. Initially struggling with depression, he found a new purpose through adaptive sports.

- **Impact**: He became a Paralympian and an advocate for accessibility in sports facilities, inspiring countless others to pursue their goals despite physical limitations.

## Table: Personal Strategies for Resilience

| Challenge | Resilience Strategy | Outcome |
|---|---|---|
| Career loss | Reimagining skills in a new field | Successful catering business |
| Physical disability | Adapting to new circumstances | Paralympic success and advocacy efforts |

*"Strength doesn't come from what you can do. It comes from overcoming the things you once thought you couldn't."* – Rikki Rogers

## Keys to Turning Challenges Into Opportunities

| *Key* | *Actionable Advice* |
|---|---|
| **Start Small** | Focus on immediate goals to build momentum. |
| **Leverage Support** | Engage family to amplify efforts. |
| **Embrace Adaptability** | Be open to change to pivot when needed. |
| **Focus on Strengths** | Use passions as a foundation for opportunities. |
| **Celebrate Wins** | Acknowledge the smallest achievements. |

**ACTIVITY:**

**Visualizing Resilience: The Ripple Effect**

Draw a central figure *diagram* representing resilience sends out ripples:

- **Inner Ripple**: Personal growth (mindset shift, new skills).

- **Middle Ripple**: Impact on immediate surroundings (family, close friends).

- **Outer Ripple**: Community-wide change (initiatives, shared success stories).

_____

_____

_____

_____

_____

_____

_____

_____

_____

_____

Resilience thrives when personal determination intersects with community support. Individuals like Mia and David inspire through their personal journeys, while small-scale efforts like neighborhood revitalizations create shared benefits that extend far beyond the initial goal. These unconventional stories of resilience remind us that even the smallest efforts can lead to extraordinary outcomes. Whether it's a crowdfunding campaign that revitalizes a business or an individual's journey to reinvent their life, the common thread is a willingness to adapt, persevere, and inspire others. Resilience isn't just about overcoming challenges; it's about creating a ripple effect that uplifts everyone around us.

*"Your strength, no matter how small, can be the spark that lights up an entire community."*

# Chapter 17:

# Spirit Cannot Be Broken

*"When you have a "why" to live for, you can bear almost any how." – Viktor Frankl*

Living purposefully is about bringing meaning and direction to your life. It's not about having every detail figured out but rather understanding what truly matters to you and letting those values guide your actions. A purposeful life fosters resilience by giving you a clear reason to persist through challenges. It provides the "why" that sustains you in the toughest of times.

Purpose acts as a foundation during difficult moments. Research from the University of Michigan highlights that people with a clear sense of purpose recover more quickly from setbacks.

A strong purpose adds context to challenges, making them feel manageable rather than overwhelming. For example, a parent working long hours may endure the strain more easily because they are motivated by their desire to provide for their children.

**Practical Steps to Live Purposefully:**

1. **Identify Core Values**: List three things that matter most to you (e.g., family, education, creativity).

_____

_____

_____

_____

_____

2. **Set Meaningful Goals**: Align your short-term and long-term goals with these values.

_____

_____

_____

_____

_____

_____

3. **Reflect and Adjust**: Regularly review your actions to ensure they reflect what you value most.

_____

_____

_____

_____

_____

_____

**Example**:

- **Value**: Helping others.

- **Goal**: Volunteer at a community center once a week.

- **Reflection**: "This gives me a sense of fulfillment and reminds me of the positive difference I can make."

**Key Insight**: Living purposefully doesn't require grand achievements. It's about finding alignment between what you value and how you act daily, even in small ways.

### Absorption of Strength

Absorbing strength means finding resilience by drawing on both external and internal resources. It involves gaining wisdom from people, experiences, and lessons, as well as building internal habits that make you stronger over time.

195

Building connections with others is one of the most important ways to strengthen resilience. When life gets tough, having someone to lean on can make all the difference. Whether it's a family member who knows exactly how to cheer you up, a friend who listens without judgment, or a mentor who offers wisdom, these relationships provide more than just comfort—they give you the tools to keep going.

Even connections with people we don't know personally, like hearing an inspiring story from a stranger or reading about someone who overcame similar struggles, can remind us that we're not alone. These moments offer fresh perspectives and encouragement, showing us that adversity isn't permanent and that others have found ways through it.

I've noticed that during my own tough times, the people around me have been my greatest resource. Sometimes it's the big gestures, like a friend stepping in to help with a problem, but other times, it's the small things—a kind word, a shared laugh, or simply knowing someone's there for me.

*Mentorship:*

A young professional struggling with career setbacks might find motivation/guidance through conversations with a mentor who has faced similar challenges and persevered.

**Learning from Experiences**

Life has a way of teaching us things, even when we're not ready to learn. Every challenge, no matter how tough or frustrating at the time, carries a lesson.

Looking back on the struggles I've faced, I realize that those moments weren't just about surviving—they were shaping me into someone stronger and more capable.

For instance, there was a time when I lost a job unexpectedly. At first, it felt like the world was crashing down. But as I moved forward, I learned how to adapt, think creatively, and find new opportunities.

Now, when I face uncertainty, I draw on the confidence I built during that tough period. I've learned to trust myself and my ability to figure things out.

When I reflect on the challenges I've overcome, I can see the skills I've picked up along the way—like patience, problem-solving, and resilience. It's a reminder that even in our hardest moments, we're growing.

The key is to take a step back, look at the big picture, and ask, "What did this teach me?"

It doesn't make the challenges easier, but it gives them purpose. And knowing that gives me the strength to handle whatever comes next.

**Activity**:

Write down three challenges you've overcome. For each, note what you learned and how it made you stronger.

_____

_____

_____

_____

_____

_____

_____

_____

_____

_____

_____

_____

_____

**Table: Turning Challenges into Strengths**

| Challenge | Lesson Learned | Strength Gained |
|---|---|---|
| Losing a job | Adaptability and perseverance | Confidence in handling uncertainty |
| Moving to a new city | Building new connections | Improved social skills |
| Facing a health issue | Prioritizing self-care | Greater appreciation for well-being |

Imagine you've just lost a job. It's a tough moment, and it's easy to feel like the rug has been pulled out from under you. But as you navigate the uncertainty, you learn to adapt and persevere. You figure out how to update your resume, explore new opportunities, and maybe even pivot to a different career path. Through that experience, you gain confidence in handling situations where there's no clear road ahead.

Now picture moving to a completely new city. At first, it's overwhelming—new streets to learn, no familiar faces, and everything feels foreign. But as you settle in, you start building connections. Maybe you join a local club, meet neighbors, or strike up conversations at work. Those efforts teach you how to connect with people and improve your social skills, making it easier to feel at home anywhere.

Finally, consider facing a health issue. It forces you to slow down and reevaluate how you're taking care of yourself. You begin to prioritize your well-being, whether it's by eating better, exercising, or simply resting when you need to.

This challenge helps you appreciate your body and health in a way you hadn't before.

Each of these situations pushes you to grow, teaching lessons that leave you stronger and better equipped for future challenges.

Internal strength comes from habits like mindfulness, gratitude, and self-reflection. These practices help you approach challenges with a clear and steady mind, allowing you to maintain focus and resolve even in difficult situations.

> *"Strength grows in the moments when you think you can't go on but keep going anyway."*

### Day-to-Day

The way you respond to everyday stressors, unexpected detours, or minor setbacks shapes your overall ability to face larger challenges.

### Practical Resilience in Action

1. **Daily Gratitude**: Reflecting on three things you're thankful for shifts your mindset toward positivity, even on difficult days.

2. **Micro-Adaptations**: Adjusting to small changes—like finding a solution to a delayed commute—builds the habit of flexibility.

3. **Self-Compassion**: Forgiving yourself for mistakes and focusing on what you can learn fosters emotional strength.

### Example:

A working parent juggling a stressful morning might pause to take a deep breath, remind themselves that it's okay to have off days, and focus on making the rest of the day better.

**Small Actions, Big Impact**

The small, consistent actions we take daily create lasting habits that reinforce resilience.

- **Taking Walks**: Regular movement reduces stress and clears the mind.

- **Connecting with Others**: A quick text or call with a friend provides emotional support.

- **Learning Something New**: Trying a new skill fosters adaptability and builds confidence.

**The Cycle of Everyday Resilience**

*1. Challenge* → *2. Reflection* → *3. Adaptation* → *4. Growth*

**How It Works:**

The cycle of everyday resilience is continuous. Challenges present opportunities to reflect, adapt, and grow, creating a feedback loop that strengthens your ability to handle future difficulties. By consciously moving through these stages, you build habits that reinforce resilience over time.

**ACTIVITY: Visual Representation:**

Sketch a circular diagram with arrows connecting each stage, symbolizing the ongoing nature of resilience. Each stage flows into the next, emphasizing growth as the outcome of intentional action.

---

---

---

---

---

---

---

---

---

---

---

---

Living a purposeful life is about having intention in your actions, even when the path ahead isn't clear. It's not about achieving perfection or always knowing the next step—it's about committing to the journey and finding meaning in it. Purpose provides a reason to keep going, even when the road gets tough. Studies published in *The Journal of Positive Psychology* show that people with a strong sense of purpose report greater happiness and mental health, even in challenging circumstances.

It isn't reserved for grand achievements. It's found in everyday actions that reflect your values.

- A **teacher** finds purpose in helping a struggling student understand a concept.

- A **nurse** feels fulfilled by comforting a patient during a stressful time.

- A **chef** finds meaning in creating meals that bring people together and foster connection.

- A **firefighter** feels pride in protecting the community and offering safety during emergencies.

- A **writer** feels fulfilled by crafting stories that inspire others or help them see the world differently.

- A **parent** experiences purpose in teaching their child important life skills and values.

- A **musician** feels joy in creating songs that comfort and uplift listeners during tough times.

- **A gardener** takes pride in cultivating plants that beautify a neighborhood or provide fresh food for the community.

- **A social worker** finds satisfaction in helping families navigate challenges and build better futures.

- **A coach** feels accomplished when mentoring youngsters to grow in skill and confidence.

- **A scientist** feels driven by conducting research that contributes to solving global problems like disease or climate change.

- **A shopkeeper** finds joy in creating a welcoming space where customers feel valued and supported.

These examples demonstrate how roles can carry extraordinary purpose, impacting individuals and communities in meaningful ways.

**Interactive Prompt**:

Write down one value that matters deeply to you. Then, write one action you can take tomorrow to honor that value.

_____

_____

_____

_____

*"The human spirit is stronger than anything that can happen to it." – C.C. Scott*

# Final Reflections:

# The Endless Road to Growth

As you complete this reading, it's essential to pause and consider what you've unearthed—not merely about resilience but about your own ability for advancement, fortitude, and transformation. This isn't the conclusion of your narrative; it's the prelude to a fresh phase, one brimming with promise and opportunity.

**Core Lessons**

1. **Resilience Is Universal**

   Every person holds the potential to rise above difficulties. Throughout histories, cultures, and experiences, resilience has been an enduring strand in human endurance and prosperity. It reminds us that while hardships may feel individual, the capability to conquer them is shared by all.

2. **Optimism Sustains Power**

   A defined objective and confidence in the future offer the drive required to withstand and persist. Optimism converts obstacles into opportunities, providing direction even during ambiguous periods.

3. **Exchanged Narratives Foster Development**

   By conveying tales of endurance, we not only establish bonds but also create waves of encouragement. Accounts of overcoming hardships reaffirm that no one faces struggles in isolation and that absorbing lessons from others can illuminate the path forward.

## Accept Your Journey

Your journey—filled with trials and triumphs—is a reflection of your fortitude. Recognizing and valuing your singular story is the first move toward unleashing your abilities. Each challenge you've endured has added depth to your essence and instruments to your toolbox. It's time to claim your narrative, acknowledging that even the smallest successes add to your evolution.

### Reflection Exercise:

Recall a difficulty you recently navigated. What understanding did it provide about yourself? How can this realization equip you to handle forthcoming challenges?

_____

_____

_____

_____

_____

_____

_____

_____

**Call to Action: Endurance in Practice**

Resilience isn't an inactive trait; it's a proactive endeavor. It isn't a stopping point; it's a perpetual expedition, continuously influenced by the hurdles we encounter and the insights we gain. The genuine measure of resilience resides not in grasping its concept but in applying it consistently—in how you handle setbacks, show compassion to yourself, and assist those nearby.

Here are actionable techniques to embed resilience into your routine and society:

- **Individual Level:** Begin a reflective journal, establish attainable objectives, and commemorate incremental progress.

- **Community Level:** Share your experiences with others, guide someone facing obstacles, or participate in a group that encourages mutual growth.

- **Global Effect:** Advocate for resilience-building habits in education, workplaces, and neighborhoods to foster a culture of collective empowerment.

**Quote to Remember:**

*"Resilience isn't simply about rebounding; it's about elevating further every time life attempts to bring you down."*

As you continue on your expedition, remember that resilience is a discipline. It flourishes through mindfulness, reinforcement, and the bravery to keep advancing. Let this work serve as the cornerstone of

your dedication to cultivating a life—and a community—where power and progress thrive, no matter the difficulties that emerge. The journey ahead is yours to define, and with resilience as your compass, it assures an odyssey worth boarding on.

# Recap

**Chapter 1: Understanding Resilience**

- Definition of resilience as the ability to recover and grow stronger through adversity.

- Exploration of the psychological, emotional, and physical aspects of resilience.

- Emphasis on resilience as a skill that can be developed over time.

- Introduction to key components: adaptability, optimism, and purpose.

**Chapter 2: The Science Behind Resilience**

- Overview of research and studies on resilience.

- Role of neuroplasticity in building mental strength.

- Importance of emotional regulation and stress management.

- Examples of how resilience impacts mental and physical health.

**Chapter 3: The Power of a Growth Mindset**

- Explanation of a growth mindset and its connection to resilience.

- How shifting perspectives can turn failures into learning opportunities.

- Strategies to cultivate a growth mindset in everyday life.

- Real-life examples of individuals thriving through setbacks.

## Chapter 4: Building Emotional Strength

- Techniques to strengthen emotional resilience, such as mindfulness and journaling.
- Role of self-compassion in managing setbacks.
- Steps to process and learn from emotional pain.
- Importance of gratitude and positivity in fostering emotional well-being.

## Chapter 5: Physical Resilience: Mind-Body Connection

- The impact of physical health on mental resilience.
- Benefits of regular exercise, proper nutrition, and sufficient sleep.
- Stress-reduction techniques like yoga and deep breathing.
- Examples of how a strong body supports a resilient mind.

## Chapter 6: The Role of Purpose in Resilience

- How a clear sense of purpose enhances resilience.
- Finding meaning in adversity and using it to fuel perseverance.
- Practical exercises to identify and align with core values.
- Inspirational stories of individuals driven by their sense of purpose.

## Chapter 7: Social Support and Community Resilience

- Importance of connections with family, friends, and mentors.
- How shared experiences and community efforts enhance collective resilience.
- Role of storytelling in fostering understanding and unity.

- Examples of resilient communities overcoming challenges together.

## Chapter 8: Navigating Change

- Strategies for adapting to life transitions and uncertainties.
- Developing flexibility and openness to new experiences.
- How to maintain stability during periods of upheaval.
- Practical exercises for navigating change with confidence.

## Chapter 9: Turning Failures into Opportunities

- Reframing failures as stepping stones to success.
- Techniques for learning from mistakes and bouncing back stronger.
- Stories of successful individuals who turned setbacks into achievements.
- Practical exercises for building resilience through failure.

## Chapter 10: Resilience in Leadership

- Characteristics of resilient leaders.
- Importance of emotional intelligence and adaptability in leadership.
- Examples of leaders who inspired resilience in their teams.
- Strategies for cultivating a resilient work environment.

## Chapter 11: Everyday Practices to Strengthen Resilience

- Daily habits to foster resilience, like gratitude journaling and mindful reflection.

- Importance of consistency in building mental and emotional strength.

- Examples of micro-actions that contribute to long-term resilience.

- Practical tips for incorporating resilience into daily routines.

## Chapter 12: Welcoming the Unknown

- Embracing uncertainty as a chance for growth.

- Shifting perspectives to see the unknown as an opportunity.

- Tools for building confidence in unpredictable situations.

- Stories of individuals who thrived despite uncertainty.

## Chapter 13: The Mindset Shift

- Transforming difficulties into challenges to overcome.

- Importance of belief systems in shaping actions and outcomes.

- Steps to develop a resilient mindset that fosters growth.

- Activities to back up beliefs with actionable steps.

## Chapter 14: Everyday Resilience—Practical Strategies

- Tools and techniques for managing day-to-day challenges.

- How small actions can create a big impact over time.

- Checklists and routines to build resilience consistently.

- Examples of practical resilience in action.

## Chapter 15: Stories of Hope and Resilience

- Narratives of individuals and communities overcoming hardships.
- Lessons from historical examples and contemporary stories.
- Importance of storytelling in inspiring resilience in others.
- Final messages of hope and encouragement.

## Chapter 16: Pledging Allegiance to Resilience Work

- The interconnected mission of self-resilience and community resilience.
- Actionable steps to strengthen resilience individually and collectively.
- Tools like the Action Pyramid and Community Resilience Map.
- Call to action for readers to share and amplify resilience in their lives.

## Chapter 17: Spirit Cannot Be Broken

- Resilience as an ongoing journey, not a destination.
- Importance of living purposefully and finding meaning in challenges.
- Drawing strength from people, experiences, and lessons.
- Motivation to embrace your story and continue building resilience daily.

# About the Author

Serah is licensed as a Certified Rehabilitation Counselor and a master's Level Clinician in her current role at Nonotuck Resource Associates Inc. Serah has worked with Children and Adults with various health challenges and diagnoses, including Autism Spectrum Disorders, Psychiatric/Mental Health Disorders, Acquired Brain Injury, and related Cognitive challenges. Serah is well-versed in Trauma Informed Care and has helped families navigate through complex Trauma that transcends across generations. Serah is a life learner and is currently pursuing a Doctorate Degree in Behavioral Health. Serah hopes to make an impact in the healthcare industry post-graduation in 2025.

Additionally, Serah is a Certified Life Coach trained in Neurolinguistics, and Brain Stimulated Wellness techniques. Serah is the owner of Limitless Success and Wellness, LLC. Through her work, Serah's intrinsic desire is to empower others to become their best version.

Serah is also an Author. Her book "Limitless Success with Serah W. Muiruri "is available on Amazon. Serah has several other books in the works, and they are expected to be available on Amazon soon.

In her spare time, Serah enjoys serving her Kenyan Community in the US, traveling, nature, and spending time with her family, especially her nieces and nephews, whom she considers her own in every sense.

www.ingramcontent.com/pod-product-compliance
Lightning Source LLC
Chambersburg PA
CBHW051514120626
46551CB00012B/914